D1611240

Reginald Brill

Reginald Brill. *Self-portrait*. Oil on canvas

Judith Bumpus

Reginald Brill

Scolar Press
in association with
Kingston University

Copyright © Kingston University 1999

Published by
Scolar Press
Gower House
Croft Road
Aldershot
Hants GU11 3HR
England
in association with
Kingston University
Knights Park
Kingston-upon-Thames
Surrey KT1 2QJ

Ashgate Publishing Company
Old Post Road
Brookfield
Vermont
05036-9704
USA

First published 1999

All rights reserved. No part of this publication may
be reproduced, stored in a retrieval system, or
transmitted in any form or by any means,
electronic, mechanical, photocopying, recording
or otherwise without the permission of the
publisher.

ISBN 1 84014 696 6

British Library Cataloguing in Publication Data
A CIP record of this book is available from
the British Library

Endpapers: Selection of illustrated envelopes
(wage payments) presented weekly by Brill to his
housekeeper Nellie Smith

Produced for the publisher by
John Taylor Book Ventures
Faringdon, Oxfordshire
Designed by Alan Bartram
Typeset by Tom Knott, Mears Ashby,
Northampton
Printed in Singapore

Sponsors

Kingston University is indebted to the following supporters of the Brill Project:

Jill Oddy
The Garden House School
London and New York
A school that places enormous importance on artistic endeavours and rejoices in the performing arts
53 Sloane Gardens
London SW1W 8ED

Carol Richards

Frère Jacques

Waterstones

Piano Nobile

Contents

Foreword
Leo Duff MA RCA
Brill Project Curator

This book pays homage to the memory of the distinguished former principal of Kingston School of Art which has since become the Faculty of Design, Kingston University. Reginald Brill had a powerful influence on the development of the school both in terms of its expansion and prestige during his time in charge and the reputation which it continues to enjoy today. Last year the Faculty of Design decided that 1999, the centenary year of Kingston College of Art, would be a splendid opportunity to celebrate Brill, both as an artist and an educator.

Brill was by all accounts a man with the presence and appearance of the serious bohemian artist, but these were combined with a calm patience and dry wit. Recollections from his staff and students focus on the personal and academic abilities he possessed to establish Kingston as a leading School of Art – alongside other reminiscences of a less formal nature.

Brill was well known and respected in the Royal Borough of Kingston-upon-Thames, not least for the development and growth of the School of Art. His opinion was sought on many matters ranging from which colour the lamp-posts in Kingston should be painted to the setting up of the collection of topographical paintings of Kingston and its environs by different artists, now known as The Brill Collection and housed in Kingston Museum.

Brill's management of the School of Art achieved remarkable results on many levels. Not only was an entire purpose-built art school opened in 1939, during a period of recession, but with an ever-increasing number of applicants over the next couple of decades, Brill was able to go on to persuade the powers-that-be to extend the school: additional studios were opened in 1961. These two buildings (plus a further extension) provided the accommodation still used by the Faculty of Design today. Students of high quality were in plentiful supply as the reputation of the school flourished, and many of them went on to further studies at The Royal Academy Schools and Royal College of Art, while others left to commence their careers as practising artists and designers. This legacy continues today: Kingston's worldwide reputation means that its graduates are sought after by such diverse enterprises as the international fashion houses Donna Karan and Calvin Klein in New York, international packaging exhibitions such as Paris Emballage, designer furniture-makers such as Hille and IKEA and film and television companies as diverse as the BBC and Disney.

Brill practised what he preached with a lively presence in the midst of the art school. He allocated himself a space in the studios to work on his own paintings, and frequently drew with his students at the drawing classes of which he was so proud. Brill spent almost thirty years at Kingston School of Art, and his output during this period was remarkably consistent. His attention to detail, and in particular the importance he attached to reference material, were meticulous. In his sketchbooks and ephemera now in the care of his family can be found exact measurements, notes and occasionally photographs taken for specific paintings. All this was in addition to the numerous drawings in sketchbooks, including many small details for a single painting, regardless of the scale of the finished piece. These references were amalgamated and scaled-up in the traditional squared manner, with Brill frequently completing several drawings and watercolours as preparation for a particular painting. Brill frequently abandoned works, even if he had already spent a great deal of time in their preparation, if they failed to meet his demanding standards. On the back of several of his large paintings which were finished can be found the beginnings of some which were abandoned.

Brill's persistence as a draughtsman paid off. In ten sketchbooks filled between 1955 and 1968 there is rarely a page removed or an unresolved drawing. Page after page shows diligent studies of even simple subjects such as gloves, chairs, balls of string. The same subject would be drawn repeatedly from different angles until he knew the form and surface to perfection. Brill used his trips abroad to work on townscapes and landscapes, always with the same controlled and disciplined approach. His forethought is much evident in these small studies. Proportion, scale and perspective were carefully observed and considered before each drawing was commenced. Paintings (and other works such as mosaics) all involved the working up from detailed reference material by means of drawings and watercolours. In his working methods Brill demonstrated great consistency, patience and control. Self-critical and modest, despite his nonchalant and sometimes arrogant air, it seems that Brill himself, although holding the practice of drawing to be of great importance and constantly pushing himself (and his students) in its improvement, did not really value his own efforts as a draughtsman at their true worth. There is no doubt, however, that he was a great craftsman when working with pen and pencil.

Along with his contemporaries William Roberts and Stanley Spencer, Brill followed the fashion of his time by setting himself a theme to pursue in his painting. 'The Martyrdom of Man' was the title Brill gave to his long-running series of paintings depicting, with acutely observed realism, local and workaday activities. Men working or resting at the road side, window cleaners, removal men, medical teams, courtroom scenes or auctions provided him with opportunities to employ his observation and draughtsmanship in a grander format. Many of his paintings were much larger than common at the time. The over-painting of several layers of colour gives Brill's oils a subtle hue, not readily noticeable at a distance. This helps give form to the characters (nearly always male) which make up his main compositions. They are given a richness not only in colour but also in expression and their communication with one another. Brill obviously had great respect for his fellow man, particularly at work, and in these compositions portrays him with much gentleness: at the same time these paintings provide important evidence of times past.

In spite of Brill's sensitivity and acute observational skills (both verbally and as a draughtsman), not to mention his reputation of being something of a ladies' man, only two works (both drawings) that I have seen contain any suggestion of sensuality: one is a drawing of a man at rest and the other simply a study of hands. In the main his subjects, although portrayed with human warmth and often earthiness, lack any sexual quality or excitement. The poise, and indeed posed, depiction of the subjects in his paintings leads to an air of peace and contemplation. No one is ever agitated or highly animated and, despite the softening of features and calmness of their poses, the people he used for his compositions remain recognisable as particular individuals.

Brill actively sought out artists to teach at Kingston who would develop new and different strands to those in his own work. As well as being of benefit to the students, the influence of his peers can also be seen across the range of techniques Brill experimented with. His unusual painted and cut card mosaics are highly successful and also reflect occasional flirtations with rather different subject matter. Compositionally these must have helped Brill with work he undertook from time to time as illustrator of book jackets (mostly thrillers), working in gouache or watercolour on a fairly small scale. The commissions for advertisements promoting Lloyds Bank (line drawings) show the working man as a rustic, somewhat patronised character, in keeping no doubt with the accompanying copy and art directors' instructions. Even so, both book jackets and newspaper advertisements clearly demonstrate Brill's craftsmanship and his ability to turn his mind to work in a variety of media and formats.

We hope that the revival of interest in Brill's work (as highlighted by the Tate Gallery's purchase of *Rest*) will lead to fresh opportunities for students at Kingston. In an environment which now includes Painting, Sculpture, Architecture, Landscape Design, Furniture, Product and Interior Design, Fashion, Graphic Design and Illustration, Brill's ethos of drawing practice, exploration and self-criticism are still most vital elements in our students' development. This academic heritage of the importance and value of drawing as established by Brill is the area we shall now, after retrospective exhibitions and publication, develop to the benefit of new students. Already students in the Faculty of Design have received support for drawing from the Fine Art dealers, Hazlitt Gooden and Fox Ltd and from Claremont Decorative and Fine Art Society.

The permanent loan of their collection to Kingston University by the Brill family is an additional benefit to our students. To display this as a Drawing Study Collection with open access to all, providing a platform for research, critical debate, comparison and inspiration for future generations, is the next stage of The Brill Project.

Former colleagues, students, friends, and owners of Reginald Brill's work, are invited to contact Kingston University.

We wish to continue gathering recollections and information concerning the life and work of Brill and to establish an archive at the Faculty of Design. Please contact:

Leo Duff
Brill Project Curator
Faculty of Design
Kingston University
Knights Park
Kingston-upon-Thames
Surrey KT1 2QJ

Reginald Brill
Judith Bumpus

'Reginald Brill was an enigma. He was like a cut gem who presented different facets at different times to different people,' Reginald Hanson recalls. As both student and teacher at Kingston School of Art Hanson knew Brill over a number of years and he articulates an impression endorsed by many others, that whatever the occasion, whoever the audience, Brill sparkled in its midst. Yet by nature he remained perplexingly elusive, reserved to a degree which was sometimes construed as an arrogant indifference to others. No-one, not even his closest friends, can say that they really knew the 'inner' Brill.

This picture presents a conundrum. By all accounts Brill was a dominant, outwardly friendly presence in Kingston. He was a tall and impressive man, with striking, bearded features, almost god-like in appearance, some would say. Certainly his air of calm, confident authority lent his personality a larger than life dimension. He has been described as an Augustus John figure and his wife Rosalie, a handsome Dorelia. Secretly Brill may even have emulated John, though he never quite achieved his Bohemian dash and flamboyance, nor his dazzling, public success as an artist on the London scene.

In the small community of Kingston Brill could, none-theless, shine and manifestly glowed with pleasure in its limelight. He spent nearly a third of his life first as Head Master, later as Principal, of the School of Art, juggling his professional responsibilities with activities to supplement his income: books, articles, reviews, lectures, examining, designs for advertisements and dust jackets, book illustration, and commissions, however humble, which came his way. It could be said that Brill was in his element in Kingston. The School was his castle and he was king: it was his own 'dung heap on which to crow & strut,' he wrote, with typical self-deprecation.[1] As a performer and would-be comedian he was an immensely attractive personality. His 'summer crits', as he swept around the painting studio uttering a spontaneous comment on each student's work, were by all accounts a *tour de force*. There is no doubt that he revelled in a position centre-stage and in his power to engage an audience with his witticisms, although that same wit could also be searing, and the hold he exerted on people could be painful if his favour were withdrawn. As the town's senior artist he was consulted on all aesthetic matters, from the choice of colour for a bridge or street furniture, to the restoration of heritage buildings. When he left Kingston, he could, with justification, feel pride in the reputation he had established for the School, and in the relationships forged with the local community and beyond.

Such was Brill's aura that his behaviour has acquired a certain mystique. A characteristic episode in his story is related by two of his students of the early 1940s, Hanson and Daphne Newington. They retain vivid recollections of a private garden party hosted at Claremont House by Sir Sydney Camm, designer of the Hawker Hurricane fighter, at which Brill, their normally sober-suited Principal, turned up in tomato-coloured trousers. Towards the end of the party Brill, with great panache, suddenly dived fully-clothed into the swimming pool, swam the length, and emerged at the other end as though nothing unusual had taken place. Such anecdotes left a colourful legacy which was remembered and discussed long after the School had undergone various transformations towards its present status as a university faculty.[2] As staff and students put it, Brill's name continued to resound in the corridors of the Knight's Park building. Yet strangely few of them, though they may have glimpsed him hard at work in his ground-floor studio, have more than a vague awareness of his art.

Brill knew in his heart of hearts that 'the only real touch-stone to success lies in the production of work'.[3] His need to earn a living, and his interest in teaching and in running the School came continually into conflict with this conviction. Yet he was never in any doubt that his art came first. In 1972, on the retirement of Wilfred Fairclough, his successor as Principal of Kingston School of Art, Brill wrote: 'This is a note of good will from the first Principal to the last Principal. A short life; our names are writ on water.'[4] Brill was determined to leave a more enduring mark for posterity.

Brill's reputation remained for many years almost entirely local, a fact only partly explained by the figurative, and for long unfashionable, nature of his art. A retrospective exhibition held in Kingston in 1985, eleven years after his death, failed to give his name the prominence it deserved. Yet it demonstrated that Realism had far from run its course and that Brill's response to the workaday world was refresh-ingly personal in its combination of humour and compassion. Since then attention to his work has grown in interested circles, culminating in 1998 in the Tate Gallery's acquisition of its first Brill, *Rest*, one of his most impressive large paintings of the mid-1950s. It was forty-two years since this picture was exhibited in the Royal Academy and returned unsold. When it goes on display in the Tate in an appropriate context, Brill should attract the fuller recognition which is due to him.

Rest has entered the National Collection at an opportune moment, a moment at which the Tate Gallery on Millbank reverts to its original role as a gallery of British art of all periods. As we revise our judgement of British twentieth-century art, reconsidering its particular qualities in relation to European and, indeed, world art, the enduring significance of traditional values in the story of modern art is increasingly, if still somewhat grudgingly, acknowledged. Brill sits firmly in a tradition of English figurative painting, which includes, among others, his near contemporaries Harold Gilman (1876-1919), Stanley Spencer (1891-1959), William Roberts (1895-1980), and his exact contemporary, and possibly his professional model within the Establishment, Thomas Monnington (1902-76). Unlike Monnington, Brill never experimented with pure abstraction. He was well aware of contemporary painting problems and of continental avant-garde developments. He occasionally explored progressive practices, absorbing what was useful to him, but like Spencer, Roberts and many others, he believed unwaveringly in the importance to art of the visible, verifiable world, and that humanity was art's essential subject.

Two sections of a *Journal*, which Brill wrote intermittently at separate periods of his life, give a vivid insight into his aims and ambitions. He wrote the first part in manuscript in Kingston between 10 January 1934 and 11 May 1954 (Fig.22). The second was composed on the typewriter presented as one of his leaving gifts from Kingston. It was written between 20 July 1962 and 20 March 1965 in Lavenham, Suffolk, where he was appointed Warden of Little Hall, a mediaeval structure, previously home to the Gayer-Anderson brothers, and bequeathed by them to Surrey County Council for use as an Artists' Hostel. The diaries contain a record of daily events, comments on work in progress and goals for the future, notes on his financial state and economic prospects. Curiously, they contain barely a handful of references to 'R.', his wife Rosalie, and never discuss her role in either his professional, or domestic, life. An adoring and tolerant partner, Rosalie's personal aspirations as an artist subserved her desire to support Brill's vocation as *the* artist. Was her exclusion the result of an egotistical nature? Towards the end of his Suffolk diary Brill expressed concern that his record might convey a false impression of vanity. 'A good deal of my time is in fact taken up with a concern for others,' he explained.[5] Although Brill wrote with a future reader in mind, and for this reason avoided intimate details, his diary entries are the nearest we come to tapping into his heart and mind.

From several reflective passages in the diaries we sense that Brill took no small satisfaction in overcoming the dis-advantages of his upbringing, and in accomplishing what he did largely as a result of his own resources and endeavours. His early retirement from Kingston in 1962 was only the second major change in his career. It was a moment to take stock and Brill was evidently gratified that, in one field at least, his name was still around. He found himself in demand as an assessor for the Board of Education's National Diploma in Design, and as an examiner both for the Institute of Education in London University and for Durham University:

Not so bad perhaps for one who had almost no formal education. I left school at the age of 13 having learnt very little. My parents having moved frequently from place to place so the schooling I did have was very confused.[6]

In a characteristic mood of analysis and self-doubt, Brill continued in the same diary entry:

By some standards I have had a successful career but I have a feeling that the big successes have eluded me. Perhaps I have been ambitious without the ruthlessness of character to achieve the bigger prizes or perhaps the bigger prizes seemed not worth being ruthless for. I have suffered from shyness and diffidence, in later years disguised behind a facade of worldliness, preferring the small gatherings to the noisier arena.[7]

The regrets which coloured Brill's retirement were tinged with bitterness towards his parents, particularly his mother, articulated for the first time on her death the same summer:

I cannot honestly say that I loved or even liked her. I have few childhood memories which endear me to her memory. The fact is that neither of my parents were fitted by nature to have children. Not for any physical hindrance but their natures were self centred and probably the comming of the children was unwelcome and interfered with their plans. Looking back on what I know of their lives, which by the way is not much, it is a tale of muddle…. Many years ago I determined to paddle my own canoe and keep clear.[8]

In Brill's resolute bid for independence it is possible, with hindsight, to see a repetition of the attitudes and actions of his father, Edward Brüll.

Edward Brüll cut himself off from home and country when he was seventeen, apparently without a backward glance. The son of Edward Brüll, a tailor, he was born on 19 March 1874, in Lemberg, now Lviv in Ukraine, but at that time part of the Polish Province of Galicia within the Austro-Hungarian Empire. The Brülls were almost certainly of German Jewish descent, members of the multi-ethnic population of immi-grants drawn to Galicia, which rapidly became Polonised.

On leaving Lemberg, Edward Brüll travelled to Lodz in the Russian part of Poland, where he spent eighteen months, probably as an apprentice tailor. When he arrived in England by way of Paris in 1893 he spoke a smattering of French, but no English. By the following year the handsome young Pole had met an English girl, Jane Norvall and, following a whirlwind romance, the wedding of Edward and Jane took place on 2 June 1895. Jane's father, Henry Norvall, ran a prospering business as a label cutter in St John Street, Clerkenwell and, although he witnessed the wedding, neither he nor his wife can have looked with any enthusiasm on their daughter's marriage to a foreigner with no obvious prospects.

Edward Brüll's restless existence as a journeyman tailor was by no means uncommon at the time. In 1895 he had a wife and son, Albert Edward (*d.*1989), to support, and no doubt undertook work in Islington with its fashionable dress and tailoring trade. By the time their second child, Edith May, was born in 1899, the family was lodging in Westminster. A year or so later they moved south of the river, this time to a recently developed suburban estate in Hither Green. There, on 6 May 1902, in rooms over Miss May West's sweet shop at 16 Springbank Road, Jane gave birth to a third and last child, Reginald Charles Brüll.

Always looking for success round the corner, Edward Brüll, now a tailor's assistant, moved on to Bath and, by 1914, to Harrogate where he rose to the position of Head Cutter for Marshall and Snelgrove. On the outbreak of World War One the family fell on hard times when Brüll was interned as an alien. It was these circumstances which must have prompted the Brülls to alter their surname to the more Anglicised form of Brill.

Reginald finished his formal schooling at thirteen when, on the strength of his artistic promise, he was awarded a scholarship to Harrogate School of Art. There, over the next two years, his art education with its strong emphasis on drawing began.

Despite air-raids, the School's work continued without interruption. Reginald pored over copies of *The Studio* which

Fig.1 Brill outside 15 Edith Villas, West Kensington, June 1925

he pronounced 'ripping' and produced competent landscape drawings from nature.[9] He clearly excelled at the School. Barely turned fifteen, he gained a first-class Certificate for Elementary School Teachers from the National Society of Art Masters for the remarkable proficiency he demonstrated in all categories of drawing from direct observation, memory and imagination.

Determined to be an artist, rather than an apprentice teacher for which he was now qualified, Brill returned in 1917 to wartime London, accepting clerical work with a City stockbroker and various jobs on Fleet Street to fund his evening classes at St Martin's School of Art. Like a fellow-student, Barnett Freedman, Brill took on commercial artwork. St Martin's laid great emphasis on its individual assessment of each student, and would have directed Brill onto a Fine Art course. It also prepared students for London County Council Scholarships, one of which took Brill to the Slade School of Fine Art.

Brill entered the Slade in October 1920, aged eighteen, and remained there until July 1923. At the time the School was a mixture of serious, older artists, such as Richard Carline, Charles Cundall, Henry Rushbury and Leonard Squirrell, most of whom had served in the war, some also as Official War Artists, and younger students such as Brill and, in the succeeding year, William Dring, Rex Whistler, Eileen Agar and Mary Potter. Thomas Monnington, the same age as Brill, overlapped by two years. He joined the Slade in 1918, and won the Rome Prize in Decorative Painting in 1923.

The School's teaching, with its insistence on demonstrable standards of draughtsmanship, fostered Brill's particular gift. Henry Tonks, appointed Slade Professor in 1917, assisted by Walter W. Russell and Philip Wilson Steer, upheld and strengthened the aim of the Slade as first and foremost 'a general School of Drawing'. He considered it his duty to teach the great principles of drawing within 'a proper under-standing of the traditions', and 'to send young painters thus armed out into the world to fight his [sic] own battle'.[10] Tonks meant that 'thus armed' they would withstand the influence of foreign fashion and develop individual feelings and expression which had not been 'tampered with'. But in the sober post-war atmosphere students were in no mood to kick over the traces and indulge in what Tonks called 'strange experiments'. They all worked, in response to Tonks' ideal, 'as if they were going to devote their lives to the highest aims of art'.[11] Brill flourished. In 1922 he was awarded Slade certificates in Figure Drawing and Painting from Life, and several prestigious prizes: First Prize for Figure Drawing, a Special Prize for a two-week Figure Drawing Composition and, jointly with Peter Brooker, the Slade Summer Compo-sition Prize for *A Landscape with Three Figures Picnicking by a Wall* (oil on canvas, 25×40 inches, Slade Coll. 5271). In his final year, he shared Second Prize with six others for Figure Drawing. Later Brill criticised 'the wretched painting instruction at the Slade', but his Summer Composition showed the degree to which he had already mastered tone.[12] His subject was a pastoral landscape, a modern *fête champêtre*, with three figures and a dog reclining on the grass under a tree, listening to a boy playing a flute.

In 1922 Brill was engaged in painting murals of a similar nature for Christopher Turnor (1873-1940), the owner of Stoke Rochford Hall, near Grantham in Lincolnshire, probably starting the work during the Slade holidays. Turnor, Chief Agricultural Executive for Lincolnshire during World War One, was engaged in many philanthropic activities in the area, and made his large Victorian country house available to educational conferences and summer schools for the Workers' Educational Association. According to Brill it was Dr Albert Mansbridge (1879-1945), the founder in 1903 of the WEA, who introduced him to Turnor.[13] Turnor was also an architect and amateur artist-craftsman, who made a number of decorative additions to the house, and invited deserving artists to carry out others.

Brill's main commission at Stoke Rochford was for Turnor's new sitting room, where he painted a tempera frieze running round three walls with views sketched on Turnor's estate. The west wall, painted in 1922, showed a pastoral landscape with trees. In 1923 Brill returned to Lincolnshire, painting another agricultural landscape on the east wall, with cattle grazing in front of the 'Ruined aerodrome at Buckminster', a contemporary version of a classical landscape. The scenes met on the north wall where Brill depicted a village nestling among hills. Turnor recorded that Brill stayed for a year 'for the sake of being in the country', and received a handsome salary of £108.[14]

Turnor was a liberal host, throwing open his house and gardens for social events. It was on one such occasion, a dance at the Hall, that Brill met his future wife, Rosalie Clarke (1903-92). She was a local girl from Grantham, the daughter of Charles Henry Clarke, a mechanical engineer. By all accounts, the attraction was immediate and mutual.

Before leaving Lincolnshire in August 1924 Brill put plans in train for the winter, which he hoped would include Rosalie Clarke, and probably took part-time teaching in London County Council Art Schools. Since the Clarkes did not actively encourage their daughter's marriage to an indigent artist-teacher, the couple eventually took matters into their own hands the following autumn. On Saturday 10 October 1925 Brill sent Rosalie a letter from his West Kensington flat at 15 Edith Villas (Fig.1), which was to be their first married home.

My Beloved
Monday morning will not be long now dearest. Your parcel has arrived & the studio is almost finished & looks good.

Our chairs have not arrived yet so if they dont come we must manage as well as we can.

Tomorrow I shall give the finishing touches to it & then I shall wait until Monday when my wife comes.

Our bed has arrived & its ever so comfortable darling. Ive just been lying on it! We shall have some wonderful times on it. It doesnt creak or make horrible noises either.

Dont forget to come on the early train if you have to dress dear – I explained all about that yesterday.[15]

With the collusion of her elder sister, Margaret, Rosalie, in the possession of a new hat, eloped to London on Monday 12 October and married Brill in Fulham Register Office. Her mother was not a little discomfited to receive a telegram in the afternoon announcing the fact.

At the time Brill was earning a precarious freelance living as a graphic artist on *Lansbury's Labour Weekly*, launched on 28 February as a new, independent Labour paper. Edith Brill was contributing short stories and it was she no doubt who introduced her brother to its editor, the Labour MP George Lansbury. Lansbury had resigned the previous December from the management of the *Daily Herald*, which he had co-founded in 1912 and which in 1922 had become Labour's official mouthpiece. Returning to his original objective Lansbury produced a broadly cultural weekly which treated a range of issues covering employment, health, welfare and education. Although Brill never became politically active, Lansbury's ideal of a humane society strengthened Brill's sympathies, and exercised a formative influence on his thinking.

It is not known when Brill started work with *Lansbury's*, but from 25 October he was making signed contributions to the paper. He did a number of large political cartoons, portraits of leading international figures in the Labour movement and, less successfully, he experimented with a comic strip featuring the put-upon 'Albert', a character who owed something to the bowler-hatted Little Man created for the *Daily Express* by 'George' Strube. Although the strip only ran for some half dozen issues, it gave the first hint of Brill's interest in taking the working man as his subject. His most arresting pen drawings comprised a remarkable series of over forty shoulder-length portraits of influential socialists. Launched with a portrait of Nikolai Lenin, the selection constituted a gallery of past heroes, as well as of living personalities. After a trial run of a few numbers, 'comrade' Brill's work was given pride of place on the paper's front page. At first Brill achieved his likenesses with bold hatching and cross-hatching. This technique changed significantly for the issue of Saturday 26 February 1926, when he realised a much subtler effect, modelling the head by means of stippling. His application of small dots to construct form was labour-intensive and could be further elaborated by blotting, and, where he required deep shadow, worked to a solid black. Brill developed the method to powerful and telling effect, and continued to refine it throughout his life in the pen and ink drawings which became a substantial part of his output.

On 26 November 1926 Brill applied for permission to compete the following year for the 1927 Rome Scholarship in the category of Decorative Painting, stimulated perhaps by Turnor's enthusiasm for Italy. The contest was completed in two stages, allowing only selected artists to compete for the finals. The requirements were based on a demanding academic tradition of carefully planned and drawn compositions, including a large cartoon. On Monday 7 February Brill heard that he was one of four finalists in the Decorative Painting category, and the only Slade student in a competition, which for a number of years had been dominated by the School's pupils. The candidates' work in the Preliminary Competitions for the Rome Scholarships was exhibited publicly in the new Imperial Gallery of Art in the Imperial Institute, South Kensington. When the Brills visited the show in mid-February Rosalie put in her diary that Brill was 'somewhat pleased with the exhibits'.[16]

The final part of the competition was to be held over the summer. In the meantime Brill completed his last commissions for *Lansbury's*, contributing on 16 July the front cover of its penultimate issue, a drawing of a young man in a cloth cap shaking the hand of an unseen figure as he set off down a long road towards the dawn. It carried the caption:

'Good-bye! Good luck! the road lies straight before you'
By REGINALD BRILL

Brill, too, pursued his independence and the following Monday began work in the Slade on his competition entry for the Rome Scholarship. The time allowed was eight weeks. Brill's subject was 'The Expulsion from Eden' for which he made careful studies from life for each of the figures, in pencil for the naked figures of Adam and Eve, and in gouache for the draped figures of angels (Plates 2 to 5 and 111). Rosalie clearly posed for all the female figures, noting in her diary that sitting for Eve was 'rather a chilly business'.[17] She was his most frequent model in the early years of their marriage and photographs show what a strikingly handsome woman she was, with strongly structured features and luxuriant long dark hair (Plates 121, 125). Domenico Marchini, possibly a professional model, posed for Adam.

A comparison of a photograph of the missing cartoon and the final painting shows that Brill made little change to his first conception. Only the landscape background was modified in part to convey the moral waste into which Adam and Eve were cast. He had not yet visited Italy, but his appreciation of Italian Renaissance painting was evident in his precise draughtsmanship and ordered design, and in his understanding of the contribution which landscape could make to his subject. There is a superficial similarity between Brill's work and Monnington's *Allegory* on the Garden of Eden, the large painting which he was required to produce in his second year as a Rome scholar. Brill may well have seen the work when Monnington was completing it in London in 1926. Under the chairmanship of D. Y. Cameron, both Monnington and Walter Russell were members of the Faculty of Painting awarding the 1927 scholarship. Sharing connections with the Slade they were likely to look favourably on work which demonstrated its ideals.

The Brills suffered continually from financial worries, and were always on the look out for opportunities to exhibit and sell work. An offer came, probably through Brill's Slade contemporary, Robert Boyd Morrison, who together with George Sheringham was advising Rupert Mason on the publication *Robes of Thespis: Costume Designs by Modern Artists*. Although the book included some famous contributors, Mason envisaged the publication as 'The Dawn of Opportunity' which would bring to light the talent of younger and unknown artists.[18] Brill was one of those who benefited, along with Paul Nash, William Dring and John Armstrong. Of his five designs Garrick's costume for Richard III had particular style and flair, but in terms of Brill's future interests Queen Elizabeth's dress, seen from the back, looked forward to his fascination with large areas of patterned fabric, notably in his drawing of *The Bibliophile*.

Robes of Thespis was not published until 1928. When Brill produced his contributions for it is unclear. Most likely he completed them before he set off for Italy, for on Friday 7 October Brill learnt that his painting had won the Rome

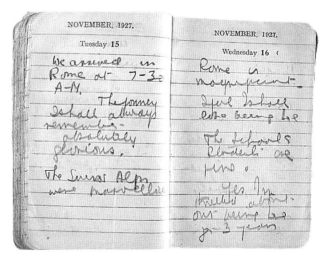

Fig.2 Rosalie and Reginald at 15 Edith Villas, prior to departure for Rome

Fig.3 Rosalie Brill's diary. Arrival in Rome, November 1927

Fig.4 The British School at Rome (Brill second from right, standing)

Scholarship of 1927 for Decorative Painting. A meeting was arranged with Evelyn Shaw, the Honorary General Secretary of the British School at Rome, and a friend and mentor to the scholars. On Saturday 5 November the Brills took the overnight train across Europe, stopping in Paris for a week to visit the Louvre, and arriving in Rome at 7.30 am on Tuesday 15 November. Voicing their mutual excitement Rosalie wrote in her diary: 'I hadn't thought that Rome could be so beautiful. Borghese Garden & the view over the parapet is very lovely. Sunshine everywhere' (Fig.3). The visit inspired in Brill a deep and enduring love of the country, its people and its language, which he worked conscientiously to acquire all his life.

Brill stayed in Rome for two years, from 15 November 1927 until the summer of 1929. Other students included George Jones, ex-Slade, the previous year's Painting Scholar, the engraver Frederick Austin, younger brother of Robert Austin, Rome Scholar in 1922, and the sculptor Harold Wilson Parker, with whom the Brills formed a particularly warm friendship, and whom Brill later brought onto the staff of Kingston School of Art. The architect, Amyas Connell (1901-80), another arrival of the previous year, also became a close friend.

Bernard Ashmole (1894-1988) was Director of the British School at Rome when Brill arrived. An expert on classical art,

he also took a lively interest in new ideas in the fine arts. He sat both to Harold Parker for a terracotta bust, and in 1928 to Brill, who painted a full-length oil portrait of Ashmole in his study examining a 'piece-cast' of a Roman head (Figs 5, 6). His most imaginative move was in commissioning Connell in 1928 to design and build him a family home in Amersham, Buckinghamshire. Set in a formal garden of Italian design, *High and Over* was the most sensationally modern house in England. While in Rome, Brill painted Connell's portrait in oil, and, in the early 1930s, invited him to teach the architectural course at Kingston.

In their first year scholars were required to travel widely in Italy, to copy selected works by Renaissance masters, paying particular attention to mural painting, and to produce a figure composition. Renewal of the scholarship into a further year depended on the strength of this first year's work. On 1 July 1928, D. Y. Cameron wrote to Shaw remarking of Brill's works that 'the influence of Italy is not yet clearly apparent in these, but I am confident Brill will develop greatly in his second year', and approving Brill's application for a second year extension.[19]

Ashmole resigned in 1928 and was replaced by the much older A. Hamilton Smith (1860-1941), recently retired from the British Museum. A third year in Rome was granted only in exceptional cases, and Smith's note to the Faculty of

Fig.5 Squared drawing for portrait of Bernard Ashmole

Fig.6 *Bernard Ashmole*. Oil on canvas 749×508 mm (29½×20 in)

Painting which accompanied Brill's application was hardly enthusiastic:

Reginald Brill has been working during the past year almost entirely in the studio, and his decorative designs do not seem to me to be based on real vital observation of Italian life.[20]

Brill's landscape paintings gave evidence of his travels in Italy, but, as observed, his main interest was in studio-based figure composition. His *Decoration* was almost certainly the painting called *The Well*, an ambitious, academic composition of six figures standing round a well. The solid, ample forms in this and in another six-figure composition prepared in Rome, *The Boat*, derived from Brill's experience of Italian Quattrocento painting.[21] The figures themselves were based on careful studies from life, mostly modelled by his wife, but the result appeared staged. In a letter to Brill of 1 July 1929

Shaw regretted that 'exceptional renewal' for a third year was not possible. Nevertheless, the Faculty praised 'the high quality' of Brill's work and the good use he had made of his opportunities as a Rome Scholar.[22]

Once back in London, lodging at Milton House, 22 Fernshaw Road, Chelsea SW3, Brill had to busy himself preparing for an exhibition of work by Rome Scholars to be held in the Imperial Gallery of Art. He was 'mainly repairing the mischief caused by the Customs and is working in Rushbury's studio,' Shaw reported in September.[23] As announced in *The Blackheath Local Guide* Brill was due to take up an appointment that autumn to teach painting in Blackheath School of Art under its new Principal, John Platt, former Principal of Leicester College of Art. If Brill accepted the job, he must have asked for leave of absence the following term. Whatever the case, in January 1930 he was off, at the invitation of the Egyptian Government, to paint the local Cairo scene and mount a selling exhibition. Brill may have taken the comment on his Rome work to heart and saw an opportunity to introduce more lively observation into his drawing.

Brill left London on 10 January for a thirteen-day journey by boat and train to Cairo. Soon after his arrival he wrote to Rosalie to say that he had to get an exhibition together in two months.[24] The experience of being plunged into a strange

place and a strange culture, with little money, and without painting materials, which took over three weeks to arrive, was both exasperating and bewildering. Brill constantly expressed his need to work, but found it difficult to get started. Although he saw wonderfully paintable scenes everywhere he was bothered by heat and dust storms, and mobbed by crowds, begging or selling, whenever he sat in the street to sketch. Away from the city Brill did many landscape drawings, avoiding from choice the usual tourist attractions, but succumbing to pressure to paint the Nile and to visit the Pyramids. He longed to get going in some of the many mosques he had visited, but had to contend with Egyptian protocol.

Im waiting for permission to work in two mosques, one of which is a wonderful place & so peaceful. In both places there is an element of risk of being turned out any moment even when I get permission & at every festival or prayer time I shall have to make myself scarce. There are at least two good paintings in one mosque & one in the other. It will be an expensive hobby for to make my position more secure I have be [sic] advised to tip the attendants & odds & ends liberally.[25]

The mixture of architectural elements, in particular, caught his eye (Plate 79): 'One finds old columns pinched from Christian churches just the same as one found Christian

Figs 7, 8 Reproduced from photographs of pen drawings of Mirrit Boutros-Ghali and Gueffry Boutros-Ghali, Cairo 1930

churches containing Roman col[umn]s in Italy. Then again there are bits of old Egyptian temples incorporated.'[26] The colours and patterns of shawls and turbans, and the street life in general fascinated him: 'Ive never seen such people. If only one could draw & paint them it would be wonderful. Some of them are a bundle of dirty rags but they wear them in such a way that they might all be kings or emperors.'[27] By good fortune an English artist invited him to share a local model in his studio. He began a small sketch of her head in oil: 'A marvellous head & wonderful colour'.[28]

The news of his arrival was announced on 7 February in *The Sphinx: The English Illustrated Weekly*, but clearly Brill's expectations of selling in an artistic climate, in which 'the work shown is bad – very bad', were diminishing.[29] As for the clientele: 'I suppose that there are actually about 20 people in Cairo who can tell a picture from a fried kipper', he reported.[30]

His success in 'finding a few interesting people' included a significant meeting with the connoisseur and collector Major Robert Grenville Gayer-Anderson, Pasha, a retired military surgeon who had been seconded to the Egyptian Army. He lived in Cairo, but returned every summer to England where he owned property in London and Lavenham with his twin brother, Colonel Thomas Gayer Gayer-Anderson. 'So probably we shall see something of him,' Brill wrote prophetically of an encounter which blossomed into his most important relationship.[31]

When Brill's first one-man show eventually opened on 23 March, it did better than anticipated, earning him enough money to take a longer route home from Alexandria, travelling to Brindisi via the Greek Islands, and from there back to England.

Over the next two years he found teaching posts in several London County Council Art Schools, including Blackheath where he taught Painting and Figure Composition two days a week. The Principal, Platt, was an enlightened and liberal man, who left Leicester to give more time to his own work, and encouraged his staff to do likewise. In 1931 Brill was one of a number of rising artists included in an exhibition in the Imperial Gallery of Art, where he showed a large oil, *La Barca* (No.195) and *Study*, in pen and ink (No.103).[32] *La Barca*, now missing, was one of the compositions initiated in Rome. It depicted six vineyard workers, three men and three women, returning wearily from their labours in a rowing boat, with two tubs of grapes (Plate 117).

Platt exhibited regularly in the Royal Academy and his example may have motivated Brill to send works there for the first time that year, two of which were hung, *Young Woman in Rome*, in tempera (No.895) and *Portrait*, in pen and ink (No.1180). The following March two of Brill's paintings were included in an exhibition of *Modern English Pictures* at the Leicester Galleries, *Long Hair* (No.101) and *Coloured Beads* (No.104). Neither picture sold and in April 1933 they re-appeared in the Galleries in Brill's first British one-man

Fig.9 July 1929

show, a selection of twenty-five paintings and drawings including portraits, a small nude, still lifes and landscapes. The subject of one of his eight oil paintings, *Unemployed* (No.13), moved him deeply and he returned to it a few years later as part of an ambitious programme of paintings on the human condition. The theme marked a decisive change in his work from academic compositions inspired by Renaissance sources to scenes of contemporary realism which had made such strong appeal in Cairo. In the critical climate of the times it was the formal qualities of Brill's work which attracted attention, rather than its content. As P. G. Konody, art critic of *The Observer*, commented: 'Mr. Brill is better in his drawing than in his oils. He has a clear conception of the effectiveness of linear arabesque.'[33] Disappointing sales and Brill's probably harsh judgement of his own painting abilities may have deterred both gallery and artist from risking another exhibition. He withdrew to the privacy of his studio where he could allow his ideas to mature to his own high standards. When he next showed his work in London, in the Royal Academy, he was fifty-one years old.

Until the Brills could afford to return to Italy after World War Two, they took their summer holidays in Britain. In the early 1930s their trips to paint landscape watercolours included South Wales, the north west of Ireland and Suffolk, probably introduced to the county by the Gayer-Andersons who lived in Lavenham. Rural life round the nearby village of Cockfield provided some of Brill's favourite subjects for a number of years. His Welsh landscapes were probably painted in the scenic surroundings of the Brecon Beacons (Plate 63), a short drive from Swansea where his sister-in-law's family lived and where, in 1931, his first nephew, David Brill, was born. In a crisply drawn view of the mountainside we sense his interest in the structural design of the landscape. The fine attention to detail was more typical of the botanical drawings he made around this period, and two years on we see him trying to work more freely. In 1933 he visited Donegal, perhaps at Albert's suggestion, where the lochs and mountains, particularly in the area around Muckish, inspired some of Brill's most spontaneous and purely painterly watercolours (Plate 66). Nowhere else did he take such obvious pleasure in capturing the richness of the landscape: the vivid, moist colours, the patterns made by the vegetation and cloudy skies, and the swiftly changing light so characteristic of this area. The textural and spatial effects he creates by dragging drier colours across the surface contrast with his known oils of this period, which like some of the Italian landscapes tended to be tonally subdued and two-dimensional in quality.

In September 1933 Brill applied to Kingston School of Art in Surrey for the vacant post of Head Master and on 10 November heard that he was the successful candidate. He took up his appointment on New Year's Day, 1934. The School of Art occupied the first floor of the Technical College in Kingston Hall Road, a fine brick building with terracotta features, opened in 1899. It was laid out with three class-rooms consisting of a large space which could be divided by a curtain, and two smaller areas, the Head Master's office which doubled as the staff-room, and a women's wash-room.[33A] The pupils had lockers, but there was otherwise no adequate storage. Art equipment was sparse, accommodation cramped, the atmosphere lackadaisical. 'There can be a good deal of tightening up,' Brill wrote in his diary during his first week, 'more enthusiasm can be imparted to the students.'[34] He diagnosed the disorganisation as being largely attribu-table to the varied quality of the staff and the absence of a clear teaching structure, but not helped by the School's untidiness. In the early months his aim was 'quite simply a place for everything & the insistance that everything should be put back in that place. The tons of useless rubbish must go.'[35] These improvements 'must have an appreciable effect on the spirit of the staff & students & consequent [sic] the quality of the work'.[36] Putting his larger plans in place took much longer than anticipated, with little encouragement from the Ministry Inspector, F. W. Burrows, who arrived unannounced in the second week of term and continued to breathe down Brill's neck until he retired from the Inspectorate in 1939.

It was one thing to shift the rubbish, another, to shift staff, one of whom, according to Burrows, was 'a bloody joke' to everyone. Brill started by organising the School into four sections: Painting, of which he took charge, Drawing, taken by John G. Lake, and the Juniors by Augustus Lunn, leaving Design to be filled by someone who, in line with Government thinking, would relate the teaching of the useful crafts to design for commerce and industry.

By the start of the next academic year Brill felt a sense of solid achievement. In place of Lake, who left to paint full-time, Brill brought in Morris Kestelman, the first of many outstanding appointments which were to give the School its high standards and reputation. Kestelman, he pronounced, 'a great success. I am being more successful too.'[37] His philosophy was: 'Decide what you want & steadily push towards it. With lots of patience it works.'[38]

By February the following year he was writing confidently of the influence he had stamped on the School: 'I have been painting all day in the life room & one could have heard a pin drop from morning till evening. Even the ticking of the clock seemed quite loud.'[39]

Despite Brill's improvements Burrows, the Inspector, delivered the ultimate put-down on 21 March 1935:

I did not agree with your appointment when it was made & I do not agree with it now.

In 1936 in a Report on the School by the Board of Education he reiterated his views about Brill's lack of experience for the job, slightly modified in recognition of his 'other personal gifts'. The general character of the School reflected Brill's artistic tolerance and this was noted in the Report which found the art teaching in general adventurous and experi-mental. The policy at Kingston of encouraging individual expression resulted in refreshing and versatile work among the advanced students in painting and drawing. Praise for the calibre of the teaching staff reflected Brill's eye for the creative ability likely to inspire students. In the autumn of 1935 the staff comprised several teachers whose qualities Brill knew from personal experience, among them Amyas Connell, brought in to teach architecture, Howard Parker, modelling, and Albert Brill, who ran a tailoring business in London, to teach Dress Design. The Report praised their professional competence, but complained that Albert's technical instruction was not 'linked to design', a charge central to its main criticism that the School 'did not march with the time'. The School was failing its students in this respect. In the Board's Art Exams in 1936 'both design candidates were unsuccessful'. Innovation and improvement were not easy to achieve. A total of 284 students were being catered for in a School designed for a hundred, and the Report's direction was intended to goad the County Council into action: 'the provision of adequate and suitable premises was urgently needed'.

In fact, plans to develop both the Technical College and the School of Art had been under discussion in the Education Committee of Surrey County Council since 1935. The site for a new art school in Knights Park was approved the following Spring, but building itself did not get under way until November 1938. Meanwhile, Brill struggled on with growing student numbers, part-time staff, and temporary accommodation. His first full-time teaching assistant, John Dawson Binns (1912–80), was finally appointed in April 1938. Binns, a brilliant twenty-five-year-old graduate of the Royal College of Art, was brought in by Brill to create a design school, and within months Brill expressed his satisfaction: 'Binns will be quite a success'.[40] It was only when the new building opened in 1939 that the School's organisation became manageable, only then, too, that Binns could realise his excitingly progressive ideas that were to make the School one of the leading centres of design teaching in the country. By then World War Two had broken out and Brill had further problems to contend with.

The themes dominating Brill's Kingston *Journal* encapsulate the tensions in his life which he was continually trying to resolve. His role as Head Master and his educational commitment increasingly absorbed his interest. Yet they threatened his real purpose as an artist. Within weeks of his arrival in Kingston he had appropriated the pottery room, when not in use, as his personal studio, but it quickly became apparent that the realities of running an art school would rarely allow free days for his own work. From the start Brill's objectives at Kingston included a private three-year plan for a series of large paintings representing aspects of contemporary life: *The Operation* (now re-titled *A Surgical Operation*, Plate 28), already well underway by the beginning of 1934; *Unemployed*, for which he had already begun to make studies; *Rural mid-day sleepers*; and a fourth picture, 'something really lively & happy'.[41] By the following year this intention had formulated itself in his mind under the title 'Martyrdom of Man'.[42] Brill never elucidated his idea, but from the work it is clear that he understood the human condition as essentially one of suffering, not in a religious cause, but in the sense that man was a martyr to life. He was vulnerable, a victim of sickness, of unemployment and consequent poverty, of hard labour resulting in physical exhaustion, but he was a hero, too, a model of stoicism, cheerful and, as such, admirable. Two years later Brill explained his purpose in terms of creating

a simple symbolism for the doings of life. The 'sleep' picture is what I mean but of course thats an easy one. What does humanity do.

It gets born
    it   eats
          sleeps
          grows & learns
          fornicates and begets (sometimes)
          works
          fights
          grows old
  and
        DIES

In the doing of the above [?] it has appetites which are satisfied or repressed.
It is happy and downcast
It esperiences fear & is brave
It is wise and foolish
It hates and loves
It is sometimes self sufficient & sometimes turns to the misteries
If there isnt enough there to keep a painter busy Ill eat my palatte.
Most of these subjects have been painted many times, most of them are covered by the religious paintings but there is surely some simple way. It will disclose itself.[43]

Over the years Brill refined this idea, devising a framework with which he sought to give fresh expression to the universal pattern of life. He never referred again to 'Martyrdom of Man', and reverted instead to calling his programme of work, as it stretched from three to five years and more, hopefully 'the Plan'. The weighty title was in any case out of keeping with Brill's jocular approach to life and with the character of his art as it evolved. The human comedy, as he conceived it, did not involve the activities of society at large, but of working people, sometimes seen as an interacting group, more often in their individual roles within a group, or simply as individual figures. In defining the artist's aim Brill once described the creative mind as prescient: artists 'are in a position to perceive, sum up and give expression to the essence of the true spirit of the time in which they live, before the real meaning of the age is recognised by most of their contemporaries'.[44] Brill's cast of characters, self-contained, separate, silent, could be seen as reflecting that sense of social fragmentation and loneliness which is identified as characterising the spirit of his time. As a loner himself and deeply introspective, despite his ostensible gregariousness, Brill detected that mood. He would have understood it though not as one of despair, but as an unavoidable condition of human existence, particularly as it affected the artist's solitary position in contemporary society. Equally Brill's men embodied a humanist aesthetic, honouring the worth of every man. 'The art of today … is still deeply rooted in the tradition of the Renaissance,' he wrote in his book *Art as a Career*.[45] And he taught his students that the tradition was still alive and meaningful in its celebration of human endeavour. All the poses that an artist required could be found in Renaissance painting, Brill told his students, but, as he also observed, the working men of his own pictures, as they leant on a spade, sat or lay down, had taken up those poses quite naturally.[46]

Brill's procedure for producing his large oil paintings relied on the academic method which he had practised since the Slade. In Kingston he began to turn his attention more seriously to painting and the analysis of colour in its relationship to form. Since he was a perfectionist, the results never lived up to his standards. He was his fiercest critic and throughout his life felt that he had to remind himself of basic procedures. Early on in his diary, he expressed his dissatisfaction with the way *The Operation* was turning out and chided himself for his mistakes.

Once and for all – or nearly all – this lesson must be learnt. It is no good painting without adequate studies. This is how it should work 1. The idea
          2. Studies
          3. Cartoon
          4. Painting
There are three main divisions –
    Design
    Form
    Colour   Firstly the main pattern
                  Secondly the breaking-up of this into the smaller parts. The fitting together of the parts to build up the large three-dimensional shape. After the colour scheme the colour of the parts will depend on the form. Painting is drawing or the explanation of form.[47]

Preparatory work on *The Operation* began in London sometime in the early 1930s, probably inspired by Henry Tonks, who trained as a surgeon at Guy's, and by the paintings of World War One, such as Stanley Spencer's *Travoys with Wounded Soldiers Arriving at a Dressing Station at Smol, Macedonia* (1919). Brill's picture shows six figures performing an operation under anaesthetic in an upstairs hospital room. His studies depended entirely on the collection of 'facts' drawn from direct observation, and of these Brill could never have enough. Later, in Kingston, he spoke of returning to the hospital to collect more. The name of the hospital has not been established and was in any case immaterial to his representation of a group of people concentrating on the task in hand.

Brill's main dissatisfaction was with the colour which he would happily have revised.

I would like to do the Operation all over again if I had the time. My mistake was not realizing the comparative coldness of the white drapery. Had I done so the whole colour would have been much more distinguished. White drapery although it conforms to the general rule of warm and cold is comparatively much colder in the lights. The lightest part is cold to begin with. Something learnt anyway – but how stupid! For years I have known this simple and elementary fact I have seen it in paintings from Ceazan [Cézanne] to Gertler & yet I have not been prevented from making a stupid error.[48]

The canvas stood around for many years and Brill may well have touched in more colour later, lending this clinical event its present decorative appearance.

Brill's aspirations for the 'Martyrdom of Man' are significant. Despite the importance of documentary evidence, the pictures were intended, as he proposed, to be emblematic.

It would please me if each succeeding picture drew away more & more from the naturalistic representation into something richer but that must come of its own accord.[49]

His immediate problem was to get the idea down in paint as precisely as possible. In that respect he found *The Operation* 'too impressionistic … the thing does not seem to have really got down to fundamentals. Its not realistic enough. I would like the Unemployed to be strictly [?] in its true realism. I shall work out each figure properly this time.'[50]

For some time Brill had been working out his ideas for *Unemployed*, or *Men on the March* as it was retitled, with the aim of starting to paint in the summer of 1934.[51] As Rosalie Brill wrote after his death: 'He had said to me that he thought this painting to be the best of his large paintings. He had much sympathy for the subject.'[52] He would have seen the unemployed on the capital's streets, and probably witnessed the Hunger Marches on London in the 1930s. As his own family struggled through the effects of the Depression, he expressed concern about the plight of his friends, such as Amyas Connell. Brill himself confided to his diary: 'Broke. Rent owing – debts – cant afford frames – no money for canvas for my next picture "Unemployed". No commissions and apparently no possibility of commissions.'[53] And some weeks later: 'This chronic hard upness is no joke'.[54]

The darkest in colour, *Unemployed* is also the most unrelievedly bleak in mood of all his paintings. Like *The Operation* the painting is based on a strong geometry. In the one, the composition induces a sense of calm, professional

Fig.10 Photograph of a plasticine figure, modelled by Brill (see page 28)

collaboration. In the other, the diagonal movement under-scores the grim resignation of the four men moving along the gutter towards the onlooker. The narrow, vertical canvas and elongated figures, the claustrophobic composition and imprisoning wall emphasise their condition. Brill was still working on both paintings in 1936, hoping to finish them by the summer. It is not clear if this aim was realised, or if he was ever completely satisfied with either. Both remained unsold at his death.

Sleep, the next large oil painting in the series, seems to have been achieved with less difficulty. Brill returned to Cockfield in the summer holidays of 1936, working on 'the Plan doing some landscape as a relaxation'. Later he wrote happily:

SLEEP completed during the summer at Cockfield. A very enjoyable & successful summer.[55]

This may be the work, now known as *Corn in the Hills* (Plate 25), shown in Brill's Retrospective Exhibition in Lavenham in the summer of 1974.[56] The curving terrain has been linked to Ireland, but it seems more likely that, by establishing a low viewpoint, he created a form which would contain the sleeping figures and suit the opulent mood of the composition.

That summer he not only completed *Sleep*, but did substantial work on preparing *Dance*, which he hoped to finish by the following summer holidays. The whereabouts of *Dance*, if indeed it still exists, is unknown. The theme fascinated Brill, partly no doubt because it contrasted excitement and activity with the state of sleep. A small gouache in the Gayer-Anderson Collection in Little Hall, Lavenham, may have been a preparatory study for this work (Plate 18). Its slender figures suggest the use of a lay figure, which we know he took away with him as an experiment.[57] Lacking models he may have persevered with this aid, as an anecdote related by Brill seems to confirm:

The window cleaner having paused to see my painting (offering me one of his two cigarettes) said 'There's not much figure about your women is there sir?'[58]

Brill hoped to complete *Dance* in time to send it to the Royal Academy in 1938. In fact, he never submitted any of these major figure compositions. Although they hung in his home in Crescent Road he may have been unhappy about staking his public reputation on them, but it is more likely that he thought large paintings were uncommercial. Whatever the case, in July 1938 he was considering another work, determined that his new summer picture on a smaller-scale should contain only two figures. It is possible that he painted, or began to paint, *Nativity at Cockfield* (Plate 26), which was forming in his mind. A pencil study of the interior of Cockfield barn shows the calves already sketched in and a bare indication of a central tableau with Mary and Joseph on either side of the manger. The simplified design and 'naive' interpretation of the Christmas story attempted to convey an atmosphere of innocent wonder, of humanity turning to 'the mysteries', as Brill set out in his scheme. On the strength of such pictures, of other scenes set in Suffolk towns and villages, and even those in Kingston, Brill's work has been likened to Stanley Spencer's vision of Cookham. The analogy is, in my view, misleading. Brill admired Spencer's single-mindedness and brilliance, as he admired Pieter Bruegel's insights into peasant life, and was fascinated by William Robert's perception of man as a machine. But he was intent on making his own discoveries and distilling an original vision. With few exceptions, Brill never gave the impression of inhabiting a place, as Spencer clearly lived his life on the divinely activated streets, gardens and rooftops of Cookham. His subjects are secular, and his eye was focused on working people, caught off-guard, not primarily on their environment. If he depicted a recognisable setting, as he did with laborious, measured precision in his paintings of Kingston Crown Court and Suffolk auction rings (Plates 38, 33, 37), it was an excuse to provide a frame for the types that gave character to these places. Brill was out of his depth with *Nativity at Cockfield*, confusing sentimentality with religious feeling as Spencer would never have done. Although Brill's subjects could be interpreted in terms of the Christian joys of work, dance, music-making, and so on, he was not a religious man and depicted a New Testament mystery uniquely in this painting. The Brills were childless and the Christ Child is Brill's only, not very convincing, representation of a baby. He preferred older children who would sit still.

As always, Brill was at ease in Cockfield and after the holidays wrote:

Painting goes ahead. Worked really hard this summer. In any reasonable times I could have turned over in my mind the serious possibilities of risking a break from school but it would be madness now.[59]

Plans for the new school were gathering momentum, providing much excitement and distraction. Brill counted on making a name for himself there. Nevertheless concern about his work continued to torment him as the fifth anniversary of his arrival in Kingston came and went:

Its incredible. Its disgusting. I believe that I could have supported myself as an artist with a little teaching. We must see what the new school brings. I would like there to make a complete change, organize home & school there is still too much drift. Organisation is the thing, but its much easier to organise other peoples affairs than ones own.[60]

As it turned out circumstances took charge of his affairs.

On 3 September 1939 war was declared. Three days later Brill, whose faith in civilisation, despite increasing threats, had refused to allow the possibility of war, wrote:

There seems to be nothing else for it but to gather up the pieces of ones shattered plans, ambitions and future and to try to rearrange them in a fresh pattern. Who knows what the future holds, if anything … And what happens to this grand new school, built up and planned with such care?[61]

Fig.11 The purpose-built Kingston School of Art, Knights Park (opened October 1939). The building is constructed around four sides of a courtyard. Painting studies were on the first floor of the far (north) side, not visible here. Sculpture studies were below. Graphic design studies were on the south side facing the river. The students' common room was on the first floor, above the entrance

As Principal, Brill was determined that the effort should not have been wasted. A month later he artfully gained a foothold in the closed building and announced:

Today I have opened the school. On this first day there are 65 full-time students in attendance. The opening has not been sanctioned and the part-time staff will not be paid. If the War Emergency Committee of the Surrey County Council decide that Art Schools in this County should not open in war time we are in the soup. Although the education officer and HMI may applaud this piracy privately I should stand on the carpet alone.[62]

When ten days later the War Emergency Committee decided that the school could open officially, Brill commented dryly:

One might write & say 'I am obliged for the information the W.E.C. sanction the opening of School of Art and propose to reopen the school last Monday week'.[63]

Brill emerged victorious from one battle and was to fight further counter-offensives against Government moves to requisition the building. Despite the loss of staff to the forces from the summer of 1940 he kept the school open and at work, even in the shelters. 'Bombs all over the place' was a daily experience after Dunkirk. During the holidays, at the request of the Air Ministry, he engaged his students in highly skilled work painting large maps, laboriously filling in fields and other details with prescribed colours, for use in RAF training. Brill took his turn at fire-watching on the School roof. If extra duties and responsibilities kept Brill worryingly from his painting, he responded philosophically: 'My only hope is to use this fallow time to define and order my ideas'.[64] He found comfort in a move in May 1940 to 1 Crescent Road which he described as 'a paradise'. 'The garden & the new house and interests form a buffer to the outside lowness of spirit and alarms.'[65]

One painting alone illustrated the strange experience of

the war years in which 'apparently only a hair line separates the normal from the most fantastic'.[66] At some point during the late 1930s Brill rented an attic studio in Avenue Road from the local postmaster, Ben Richardson, one of his golfing partners. The narrow space between this house and the next was the subject of a gouache showing a German bomber being shot down by a Spitfire during a daytime raid on Kingston in 1943. This scene became the location for *The Nightmare* (Plates 48, 49), an exceptional subject in his work. The sequence of images from the first watercolour drawing to the oil shows how the memory grew in his imagination, vividly transforming the thrills of war into fears which took on sinister overtones in night-time dreams.

The period immediately after the war was a difficult one of readjustment. While Brill, frustrated because of the lack of opportunity to do his art, strained to break away and be independent, new problems hemmed him in. The organisation of the School was bugged by a repetition of the problems he thought had been overcome by the move to a new building. A record number of students enrolled for the session 1945-46, and by December there was a waiting list for the first time ever of thirty full-time students. By 1947, members of the School, far from rattling around 'like peas in a pod', as the Principal of Wimbledon, Gerald Cooper expressed it, had once again to tolerate an 'urgent need for the provision of additional accommodation'.[67] Three years later in 1950 hopes of settling the problem by building an extension were deferred due to the severe post-war economic and building difficulties. No doubt these discouragements exacerbated the disappointments in Brill's teaching career, for early in 1949 he wrote:

Attempts to leave Kingston have been unsuccessful.
Regent St. Polytechnic – interview
Edinburgh College of Art – nothing
L.C.C. Central School – interview
Royal College of Art – interview
The Slade is vacant but the appointment seems to be in process of consideration privately. There seems to be little prospect.[68]

He could, however, count one tangible success: the publication in 1946 of *Modern Painting and its Roots in European Tradition*, which contained a summary of his thinking about the figurative tradition in Western art and its contemporary significance in the work of Spencer, Edward Burra, Rodrigo Moynihan and others. 'Artists now are as much influenced by their predecessors as they ever were,' he wrote.[69] While he abhorred the 'art nonsense' of the avant-garde, he sustained a longstanding admiration for Picasso, who in his classical phase expressed Brill's own ideas about drawing and painting.

Brill's approach to the subject of modern art in this book is fair-minded almost to the point of dullness. Yet from the mid-1930s at least Brill was in demand as a lively and provocative speaker on themes such as 'Is Modern Art Bogus?' and 'The Truth about Modern Art'. As he established his position in the School and his home in Kingston, he found

Figs 12, 13 The Principal, his office (Room 53, Knights Park)

himself swept, not disagreeably, into the life of the community.[70] His confidence grew as he discovered both his powers of persuasion and his talent to entertain. From 1940 until 1959 he was a popular member of the Rotary Club. He lectured to the Kingston Round Table. He proposed and opposed motions in the Kingston Debating Society. He served as official painter, documenting His Worship the Mayor and Town Clerk with Macebearer in solemn procession at the Proclamation of Queen Elizabeth II, his first public commission from the Borough (Plate 29). Later that year he was appointed honorary artistic adviser to Kingston's celebrations for the Coronation in 1953. His opinions, sought after and respected, have since become legendary. At the Reception in the Guildhall to celebrate the refurbishment of the Market Place in July 1962, Brill reportedly ended his speech with the pointedly ambiguous phrase '... and I'm sure the people of this Royal Borough will get the town they deserve'. His remark may well have made veiled reference to rapid changes in the town, as post-war building swept away familiar landmarks. It was during Brill's time as secretary of the Rotary Club, 1953-55, that he conceived the idea of forming a pictorial record of Kingston in the British topographical tradition. Views were commissioned from established artists on the Kingston staff, and the Rotary Club stepped in to support the scheme as part of their Golden Jubilee celebrations. Funds were raised annually to commission drawings until 1971 when the scheme lapsed. In 1997 it was relaunched as 'The Brill Collection' in recognition of his enterprising patronage.

Brill's personal standing in the Borough was the key to the strong ties between the School and the community. He regretted the disappearance of the private patron, and whenever a piece of design was required he involved his students, whether in painting murals for a local school, or in helping with Kingston's contribution, under Eric Brown and Peter Chamberlin, to the Festival of Britain on the South Bank in 1951. Brill's main creation, assisted by two students, was a Seaside Promenade about fifteen feet long with a toy-size funfair, houses and other buildings all constructed out of tin (Figs 14, 15).

That summer Brill made the first of many return visits to Italy with his wife, to draw and collect reference material for future paintings. A detailed study of buildings in pen and wash inscribed 'Albergo Cristallo Bologna 1951' is typical of his architectural interests. He worked up another drawing into an oil painting, *Siena*, his only work hung in the Royal Academy in 1953 (No.452, possibly repainted), and his first exhibit there for twelve years. On 25 September it was returned to him unsold, prompting the usual self-critical appraisal:

In the exhibition it looked trivial ... it is too tight and too small in feeling. I must pumice-stone it down and completely repaint. I must not paint too tight. Larger brushes and much more freely especially in the beginning. The whole design must grow more slowly. Form must be more losely indicated & let harden up naturally.[71]

A favourite view of Siena, one which Brill repeated several times in oil and in the paper mosaics he devised, featured La Torre de Magnia on the Palazzo Pubblico (Plate 54).

Following his own advice he whittled away extraneous detail from his sketches, selected and compressed the dominant features into a synthetic construction of shapes, colours and textured surfaces. The result was an idealised memory of jumbled houses, rooftops, spires and towers, reorganised with poster-like appeal.

At the time Brill expressed his intention of painting more large-scale compositions. A vertical, four-figure composition, *Rural Road Works*, was already in preparation, developing a theme found eleven years previously. Four labourers stop for a lunch break by the roadside. Two are finishing their meal, one eating out of a page torn from the *Surrey Comet*, a china jug and teacup beside him. An older man in a shapeless felt hat stares at us, slightly pop-eyed. A fourth lies stretched out, dead to the world. With this work the virtually all-male cast of Brill people begins to make its appearance, cloth-capped, heavy-limbed and big-booted. Brill said that you could tell everything about a man from his boots. The men are not caricatures. They are very recognisably individuals, closely observed with sympathy and humour.

Brill framed the picture when it was near completion, a practice he resorted to when making final, difficult, adjustments. The work was eventually exhibited in the Royal Academy in 1955 (No.629), together with a drawing for *Midday* (No.999). As he was working on his painting of the road menders Brill expressed his intention of starting on 'something really good that will embody recent conclusions. I want to trace my interest in Byzantine, Sieneese, simplification to essentials & this I would like to do in my next painting.'[72] His next large oil was *Rest* (Plate 43 and dustjacket), which took a similar theme depicting four builders having a siesta, and was hung in the RA the following year. The carefully-wrought surface, less embroidered than in *Rural Road Works*, is shot through with a jewel-like interplay of hues, which Brill applied with small brushes. Its unified effect shows how accomplished Brill had become both at simplifying his subject in paint and, by his superb handling of colour, at sustaining interest throughout the canvas.

Everyday activities in Kingston continued to provide inspiration for Brill's post-war work. From the late 1950s he began working exclusively on hardboard, a support which, despite some disadvantages, he recommended. In another experimental move he revised the ideas from which *Unemployed* acquired its emotional charge. He introduced a sombre range of tones as a foil to startling accents of colour, and started elongating his figures, giving them a strangely distorted, El Greco-like, intensity. *Linemen*, a large vertical oil of three men in a canvas cabin testing the telephone lines, was among the earliest. (Exhib. RA 1958, Plates 40, 41). On a related theme, *Philosopher*, a pen and ink drawing, portrays a watchman in his hut, reading and thinking (Fig.18). The figure of the philosophic watchman may well have been inspired by the droll character created by the writer W. W. Jacobs (1863-1943), a very popular author of short stories

Figs 14, 15 Festival of Britain, Battersea Park. Kingston School
of Art's scale model (above) and final version at opening, 1951

in the late nineteenth and early part of the twentieth century, whose portrait Brill painted. Although their sympathies came from opposite sides of the social and political spectrum, they shared a genuine compassion for their fellow-men. In the eloquent re-creation of characters such as the watchman Brill found both his subject and his voice. He always worked from the particular, but his people stood for universal types, identified only by their place of work, or activity: *Minor operation*, *The kitchen*, a domestic scene drawn in his own home in 1 Crescent Road, *Window cleaner*, *The sleeping gardener*, *Dustman*, the removal men in *Pantechnicon*, a jury sitting in

Fig.16 *Window cleaner on bicycle* (Unfinished drawing showing Brill's stipple in use of pen and ink)

Fig.17 *Window cleaner with ladder*

the panelled courtroom in Kingston Crown Court (Plates 38, 39). Each member of the jury, and even the usher and the weary court clerk, are given cameo parts in the scenario. Brill's genius lay in his painstaking documentation of character and, occasionally, milieu, so that with time these paintings have assumed the air of period pieces. They were Brill's personal contribution to preserving the country's history.

This development had an interesting spin-off when Brill received a commission from Lloyds Bank to contribute designs to their prestige advertising series (Figs 31, 32). In 1957 his drawing of a gardener asleep in a wheelbarrow carried a quotation from Voltaire's *Candide*, 'but we must cultivate our garden'. With its rustic theme and oblique message, the advertisement was clearly aimed at an urbane and cultured readership of newspapers such as *The Times*, and other quality broadsheets. The image must have been successful for the following year three more of Brill's drawings appeared: 'If you want a thing done well'. 'Farewell to The Big House and the tea-pot hoard', and 'Workers of the world arise'. 'The Lady was a tramophile' was listed as a subject, but not illustrated. All three were accompanied by tongue-in-cheek narratives penned by an unidentified 'J.M.'

The fact that Brill was able to set aside time to work after the war was a mark of his ability to organise and delegate. If he became a rather less familiar figure in the studios, his leadership was nonetheless effective. He devoted as much energy to pushing through the building of an extension as to his painting. Many people have paid tribute to Brill's skills as a good politician, to his canny ways of getting things done with a combination of charm and manipulation, to the great benefit of the School. By 1959 the new building, designed by the County Architect J. Harrison, was under way, and was finally opened on Tuesday 17 October 1961 by Sir Charles Wheeler, President of the Royal Academy of Arts (Fig.35). Sir Charles described Kingston as one of the best art schools in the country and paid highest tribute to Brill when he reportedly said:

You can pay a man a salary and get his service. But you cannot pay a man in pounds for the devotion which he has given to this School.

Through sheer force of character and will Brill established the ethos and high reputation of the School of Art at a particular period in its history. By the time the revolutionary changes in art school education were introduced in 1963, the period had, to a large extent, run its course and Brill had left. For the opening coincided with the announcement that Brill would retire as Principal of Kingston School of Art in July 1962, to take up his new appointment as Warden of the Gayer-Anderson Hostel for Art Students in Lavenham.

Brill was returning to an area he had visited over many years, had painted and grown to love. Typically, he quizzed himself: 'Is this escapism? Is it a retreat from life? Are all the vital chaps tearing about London, seeing people, making useful contacts? Is one in a backwater? The answer is NO.'[73] Town life had become dehumanised because, he felt, there are too many humans. In his diary entry for 20 July 1962 Brill speculated on his change of status and what the future held for him:

certainly I cannot imagine a more fortunate situation in which to find oneself. A roof over ones head, food provided, and people to look after one, and enough money for reasonable needs. Given ten productive years if I have anything to say I should be able to say it.

The theme on which Brill spoke eloquently in his drawings and paintings focused again on local life:

There is no lack of subject matter. Almost every day something shines out asking to be recorded. The Gardener at the

incinerator with the smoke billowing around his [him?] made me grab a pencil [y]esterday.[74]

He was under no illusions about the fashionability of his interests, but remained convinced that he must pursue his own course, now with 'a clearer direction and relationship between each painting ... so that one will have a feeling of steady progression along a road, narrow perhaps but deep ...

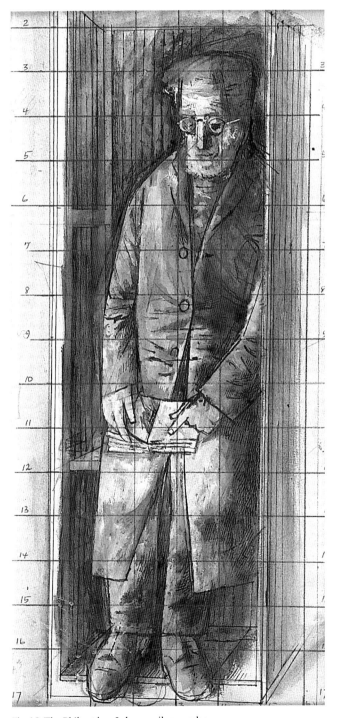

Fig.18 *The Philosopher*. Ink, pencil, gouache

Fig.19 Mrs Bidmead, Chairman of Governors (centre), Rosalie and Reginald Brill on the occasion of Brill's retirement, July 1962

my artistic activities must surely be based on a study of human behaviour.'[75]

His subjects were, as he said, invitingly to hand: the bell-ringers in Lavenham Parish Church, the Salvation Army band, Morris dancers, the village fête, the cattle markets in King's Lynn, Bury St Edmunds, and Sudbury with its peripheral junk stalls. In his meticulously measured drawings of the auction rings Brill captured the authentic setting for the ritual inspections and bidding, and occasional wheeling and dealing. The business of collecting and sifting this information was so painfully slow that he became disgusted with his progress, and had to issue himself with a reminder that:

I cannot get quick results and that for me the longest way round is the shortest way there. Acting on this principle I am engaged in making a model in order to make a drawing. I want to make a large drawing of three men in a railway carriage so I have constructed a model one eighth scale of the interior of the carriage and propose now to make figures of plasticiene (?). If this approach works there is no reason why I should not make a model every time I compose figures in space. We will see.[76]

'Must' nearly always accompanied the instructions and advice he repeatedly gave himself, followed with equal frequency by a note of uncertainty: 'We shall see'. Brill's plans of campaign to start and finish certain paintings and drawings rarely ran to programme. He was a perfectionist, beset by second, third and fourth thoughts and a fear of failure, always up before the stern self-critic. But the forgiving alter-ego would rise to his defence: 'Don't be impatient please. Judge the output on a half years work at least.'[77]

At one point Brill conceived a grand Spencerian vision of hundreds of figures. Would it be a composite picture of the inhabitants of Lavenham, he speculated, 'or would it be some dramatic end of the world kind of thing'.[78] Although he painted a multi-figured scene in Lavenham Market Place, the need to produce affordable pictures restrained him.

He fell back on small, humorous studies of local characters, landscapes sketched on his many trips to Italy, Puffin Island, and elsewhere, buildings, and ready-made still lifes of the big buoys at Harwich, a surprising, but perfect, subject for his explorations of colour.

When Brill admitted that 'my strong technical card is draughtsmanship' he echoed Konody's assessment thirty years back. 'I have been unable to reconcile this with paint-ing,' he confessed, 'but it may be I am finding the way.'[79] Brill may have pressed unnecessarily for a reconciliation. His large monochrome, ink and wash drawings, such as *The bibliophile*, *The critic*, and his self-portrait in the Library of Little Hall, are remarkably strong, highly personal creations in their own right, absorbing as much time and thought as his painting. It is possible that the dual nature of his work was not fully appreciated by his critics, and may partly account for the fact that he failed to achieve his ambition to be elected a member of the Royal Academy.

For some reason, whether through diffidence, or because of a fundamental dislike of joining a group, Brill never aligned himself with any other exhibiting societies in London. It is inconceivable that he was ignorant of their importance in attracting public and critical attention. In Suffolk he was drawn into local activities contributing to shows of East Anglian artists, accepting the Presidency of the Suffolk Art Society, and joining the committee of Gainsborough's House Society in Sudbury.[80] He showed in several mixed exhibitions in Gainsborough's House and was given a solo exhibition by Gainsborough's House Society in 1968.[81] Besides local residents and the American visitors to Lavenham, Brill's patrons were limited to frequenters of the Academy's summer exhibition. While they bought his smaller work enthusiastically, it was not their task to promote him. For that Brill needed the advocacy of publicists and fellow artists.

Throughout his career Brill's most important showcase remained the Academy's annual Exhibition. He had his first two works accepted in 1931, and, after a gap of twenty-one years, submitted three paintings or drawings regularly until his death in 1974. In all he showed fifty-nine drawings and paintings during his life. By 1960 Brill's chance of being elected an Associate of the Royal Academy looked as though it might be on the cards. It was not to be. His forthright, often barbed, remarks, may, it seems, have lost him vital support. In 1965 he had not given up hope of attaining his goal, noting on 20 March:

There is still just a chance of election to the R.A. altho this cannot be counted upon. With an assured right of exhibiting five major works each year I should be in clover and this might supply the challenge I need.[82]

In the event one of the 'big successes' continued to elude him, but in other respects he was already living in clover in Lavenham.

As Brill noted in his diary, the seeds of opportunity were sown in September 1942:

Fig.20 Brill and kitten (Tim) at Little Hall, Lavenham 1962

Fig.21 The garden, Little Hall

Spent the weekend at the Little Hall Lavenham. T.G. and John (the Colonel & the Major) wish to leave the house and contents for the use of young artists.[83] I put up a proposition that the house might in effect become an annex of Kingston School of Art and much to my surprise I must admit the suggestion has been taken very seriously.[84]

The proposal was put to the Education Committee of Surrey County Council, and Brill personally escorted a deputation to see Little Hall for themselves. He was delighted with the success of this initiative: 'It was a personal triumph for me & I enjoyed it all'.[85]

The upshot was that the Council accepted the Gayer-Andersons' offer to bequeath their house, fully-furnished with art treasures, two additional cottages, and an endowment of £3,000 for the use of students of Surrey Art Schools, and of the Slade. A Deed of Gift was accordingly drawn up by the brothers on 6 June 1945, and, in 1960, a Governing Body constituted for the Hostel. The properties became vested in Surrey Council on Colonel Gayer-Anderson's death on 10 June 1960, and the following year Brill was appointed as a resident married warden.[86]

The protracted refurbishment of Little Hall meant that the hostel did not open its doors to students until 5 February 1963, but by September that year Brill reported that fifty-four students, all from Surrey Art Schools, had visited the hostel, that arrangements were working well and that the students had been well accepted by the village (Figs 20, 21).

In 1965 a major change took place in the Council when the Metropolitan boundaries were extended and a large area of Surrey, 37.2 per cent of its population, including Kingston, was transferred to Greater London. In effect this meant that Surrey relinquished three of its art schools, Kingston, Wimbledon and Sutton, and in consequence Lavenham lost its main supply of students. Numbers had, in fact, been falling off, and for Brill, who enjoyed passing on his knowledge of Italian, but who was impatient with students' 'bohemian muddle', their lack of any plan or objective, and their limited dinner table conversation, 'this quiet spell has been very pleasant'.[87]

By 1968 the Council was very concerned about the cost of maintaining the Hostel. Under the Deed of Gift it had powers to dispose of it, but, in order to honour an agreement to give long-term notice to the Warden and domestic staff of any changes affecting their position, the Council decided to allow the Hostel to continue until the end of that summer.

The terms of the 1944 Deed of Gift were modified in a Variation Deed drawn up on 6 October 1958. It was stated that, if the premises should cease to be serviceable, the whole property and its contents could be offered first to the National Trust and then to the Society for the Protection of Ancient Buildings, to be maintained by one or other in perpetuity. If both declined, it should be offered to another artistic or charitable body, preferably local to Suffolk. When neither the Society for the Protection of Ancient Buildings nor the National Trust were able to accept the gift, the offer was made to, and in 1973 accepted by, the newly established Suffolk Building Preservation Trust Ltd. The following spring a great deal of heated feeling was generated in the village by an emotional article published on 18 April in the *Suffolk Free Press*. A photograph of seventy-one-year-old Brill standing arm in arm with his wife Rosalie outside Little Hall was placed above a dramatic headline:

'Humiliating' terms for noted artist

Sixty-two-year-old artist [sic] Reginald Brill, who has been forced out of the wardenship of Lavenham's Little Hall by a 'bolt out of the blue' legal move has aroused the sympathy of villagers who fear he is being harassed by the hall's new owners – the Suffolk Building Preservations [sic] Trust.

Henry Engleheart, Chairman of the Board of Trustees, was presented as the hard-hearted monster of the show, delivering 'ill-treatment' and forcing Brill 'who had originally expected the Little Hall to be his home for life … to move out in three months'.

A week later, on 25 April, the *Suffolk Free Press* published a letter to the Editor from Henry Engleheart. It was a calm and measured response to the accusations, setting the record straight and pointing out that the Trust's timely move reflected the Gayer-Andersons' intentions that the house and its contents should be maintained for the enjoyment of visitors. The news had not come out of the blue. The Hostel had in fact been closed by Surrey County Council in 1969. 'At no time was Mr Brill asked to leave in three months.' The Trust generously made Brill a licensee, requesting a contribution towards the running costs. What may have triggered the storm was the formal letter sent to Brill by the Trust. According to Engleheart, Brill 'bristled' at the legal language in which the solicitors' arrangement was couched. Brill was probably more deeply upset at the thought of moving and by the inevitable disruptions caused to his established way of life than he was prepared to admit. In public, though, he was reasonable and the difficulties were resolved. Engleheart sent an advance copy of his letter to Brill who, ever the diplomat, replied on 22 April, thanking him and saying: 'I hope the Press will now drop it'.

Brill died less than two months later on 14 June. There are some who still insist that the intervention of the Trust 'killed Brill'. The shock of his reversed fortunes may have done. Friends recall Brill telling them that the Gayer-Andersons had wanted to leave Little Hall to him, and it was at his public-spirited suggestion that they offered it to Surrey for the creation of a Landscape School. There is nothing in Brill's diary, nor in the Gayer-Andersons' will to confirm or deny this interpretation. If true his misapprehension must have increased his sense of injury and disappointment. He had acted like a squire of the manor and savoured every moment of it. As his dealer, Ronald McCausland-White said, Brill had no plans for the future.[88] Now he was suddenly faced with setting up home from scratch, returning to

something like the 'hard-upness' he thought he had left behind for good. He had given himself ten years in 1962 to say what he had to say. He may well have felt, looking self-critically round his Retrospective Exhibition, which opened on 25 May, that he had said his say.[89] The world of the working people of Suffolk, the very stuff of his painting, was ageing and fast disappearing. The texture and meaning of its way of life was changing irreversibly. Lavenham was starting to become a curiosity, a Little Old World Village of second homes and advancing tourism. We can only speculate on Brill's private thoughts. Certainly, those who remember him at this period discerned his dissatisfaction with what he had accomplished, but then he had always been the severest judge of himself.

When Nellie Smith, the Brills' loyal housekeeper for twelve years, said good-night to Mr Brill on the evening of 13 June she recalls a look of intense weariness on his face. The next morning Rosalie rose early to make tea. When she returned to the bedroom, she discovered that he had died of a heart attack.

The funeral took place in the Parish Church of St Peter and St Paul, followed by interment in the nearby burial ground. Gathered together for the occasion were family and friends, representatives of official bodies, and the local people whose idiosyncrasies and pattern of life Brill immortalised.

1 *Journal*, 5 June 1940. Brill's two diaries belong to the Brill Estate. In quotations from them I have retained Brill's spelling and punctuation.
2 In 1965 the School of Art was redesignated a College, which in 1970 was amalgamated with the College of Technology, becoming the Division of Design within Kingston Polytechnic. The Division of Design was reorganised as the Faculty of Design in 1987 and retained this description when the Polytechnic was redesignated a University in 1992.
3 *Journal*, 23 September 1942.
4 Letter from RB, 12 July 1972 (Private Collection). Fairclough was redesignated Principal of the College of Art in 1965, and in 1970 Assistant Director of Kingston Polytechnic and Head of the Division of Design.
5 *Journal*, 7 January 1965.
6 Ibid., 20 July 1962.
7 Ibid.
8 Ibid., 1 September 1962.
9 Letter RB to his sister, Edith (Edie), 7 May 1916 (Private Collection).
10 UCL, Slade Committee Minutes, Report, 1918, and 13 June 1922. Quoted in Stephen Chaplin, *A Slade School of Fine Art Archive Reader: a compendium of documents 1868-1975 in University College London* (Unpublished MS, 1998, UCL Library, Manuscripts Room), Vol.2, Chapter 7, Sections 7:3 and 7:4.
11 Ibid., 1918.
12 *Journal*, 1 March 1934.
13 Copy of letter RB to Ed., *Sunday Times*, 25 October 1950 (Brill Estate).
14 Information derived from C. Turnor, *Stoke Rochford 1915* and his diary and account book (Unpublished MSS, Private Collection).
15 Letter RB to Rosalie Clarke, 10 October 1925 (Brill Estate).
16 Rosalie Brill's diary, 19 February 1927 (Brill Estate).
17 Ibid., 19 July 1927.

18 Rupert Mason, and (eds) G. Sheringham, R. B. Morrison, *Robes of Thespis: Costume Designs by Modern Artists* (London, 1928), p.vii.
19 British School at Rome Archive.
20 Ibid. Brill's application was received 29 May 1929 and forwarded to the Faculty 27 June 1929.
21 *The Boat* was retitled *La Barca* when it was exhibited in 1931 in the Imperial Gallery of Art. A full-size, unfinished study for this painting exists on the reverse of *The Operation*.
22 The British School at Rome, Report, 1931, p.25.
23 Copy of letter from Shaw, September 1929 (British School at Rome Archive).
24 Letter RB to Rosalie, 23 January 1930 (Brill Estate).
25 Letter RB to Rosalie, 27 January 1930 (Brill Estate).
26 Letter RB to Rosalie, 1930 (Brill Estate).
27 Letter RB to Rosalie, 27 January 1930 (Brill Estate).
28 Letter RB to Rosalie, 7 February 1930 (Brill Estate).
29 Ibid.
30 Letter RB to Rosalie, 27 March 1930 (Brill Estate).
31 Letter RB to Rosalie, 13 March 1930 (Brill Estate).
32 *Exhibition of Paintings, Drawings, Engravings and Small Sculpture by Artists Resident in Great Britain and the Dominions*, Imperial Gallery of Art, Imperial Institute, South Kensington, 28 March - 27 June 1931. The Gallery was instituted in connection with the British School at Rome for the display of work by contemporary artists throughout the Empire.
33 *The Observer*, 2 April 1933.
33A As described to the author by Lena Cooke, student 1933-7.
34 *Journal*, 10 January 1934.
35 Ibid., 30 November 1934.
36 Ibid.
37 Ibid., 7 November 1934.
38 Ibid.
39 Ibid., 12 February 1935.
40 Ibid., 4 July 1938.
41 Ibid., 22 January 1934.
42 Ibid., 29 May 1935.
43 Ibid., 7 June 1937.
44 Reginald Brill, *Modern Painting and its Roots in European Tradition* (London, 1946), p.19.
45 Reginald Brill, *Art as a Career* (London, 1962), p.25.
46 As related by Reginald Hanson.
47 *Journal*, 11 June 1934
48 Ibid., 22 March 1934.
49 Ibid., 22 January 1934.
50 Ibid., 6 February 1934.
51 Brill frequently retitled work. From the handling this is an early work, exhibited it seems for the first time as *Men on the March* (No.70) in *Reginald Brill 1902-1974 A Retrospect Exhibition*, Phoenix Gallery, Lavenham, 26 April – 10 May, 1975.
52 Letter from Rosalie Brill, 22 May 1975 (Private Collection).
53 *Journal*, 9 May 1934.
54 Ibid., 28 May 1934.
55 Ibid., 4 December 1936.
56 *Reginald Brill: Retrospective Exhibition*, Phoenix Gallery, Lavenham, 25 May – 8 June 1974, No.19.
57 *Journal*, 5 July 1937.
58 Ibid., 9 March 1938.
59 Ibid., September 1938.
60 Ibid., 9 January 1939.
61 Ibid., 6 September 1939.
62 Ibid., 9 October 1939.
63 Ibid., 19 October 1939.
64 Ibid., 6 May 1941.
65 Ibid., June 1940.
66 Ibid.
67 Surrey County Council, Education Committee, Minutes, 16 December 1947, p.1539.
68 *Journal*, 7 January 1949.
69 Op. cit., p.19.
70 The Brills moved from Fulham to 6B Palace Road, Kingston, in late April 1937.
71 *Journal*, 25 September 1953.
72 Ibid., 23 September 1942.
73 Ibid., 12 October 1962.
74 Ibid., 3 November 1962.
75 Ibid., 22 August 1962.
76 Ibid., 6 June 1963.
77 Ibid., 11 November 1962.
78 Ibid., 28 August 1962.
79 Ibid., 13 November 1963.
80 Brill joined the Management Committee of Gainsborough's House Society on 18 March 1965.
81 Ex. *Reginald Brill Paintings*, Gainsborough's House Society, Sudbury, 6-25 August 1968.
82 *Journal*, 20 March 1965.
83 'T.G.' referred to Colonel Thomas Gayer Gayer-Anderson. By 'John' Brill may have meant the Colonel's twin brother Major Robert Grenville Gayer-Anderson, Pasha, but as he referred later, on 1 October, to 'John (Major Gayer Anderson)' it is likely that the person in question was the Gayer-Andersons' adopted son, John Gayer-Anderson.
84 *Journal*, 23 September 1942.
85 Ibid., 10 November 1942.
86 Surrey County Council, Education Committee, Minutes, 2 May 1961.
87 *Journal*, 10 January 1965.
88 As related to the author by McCausland-White's assistant, Ann Gurling.
89 See n.56.

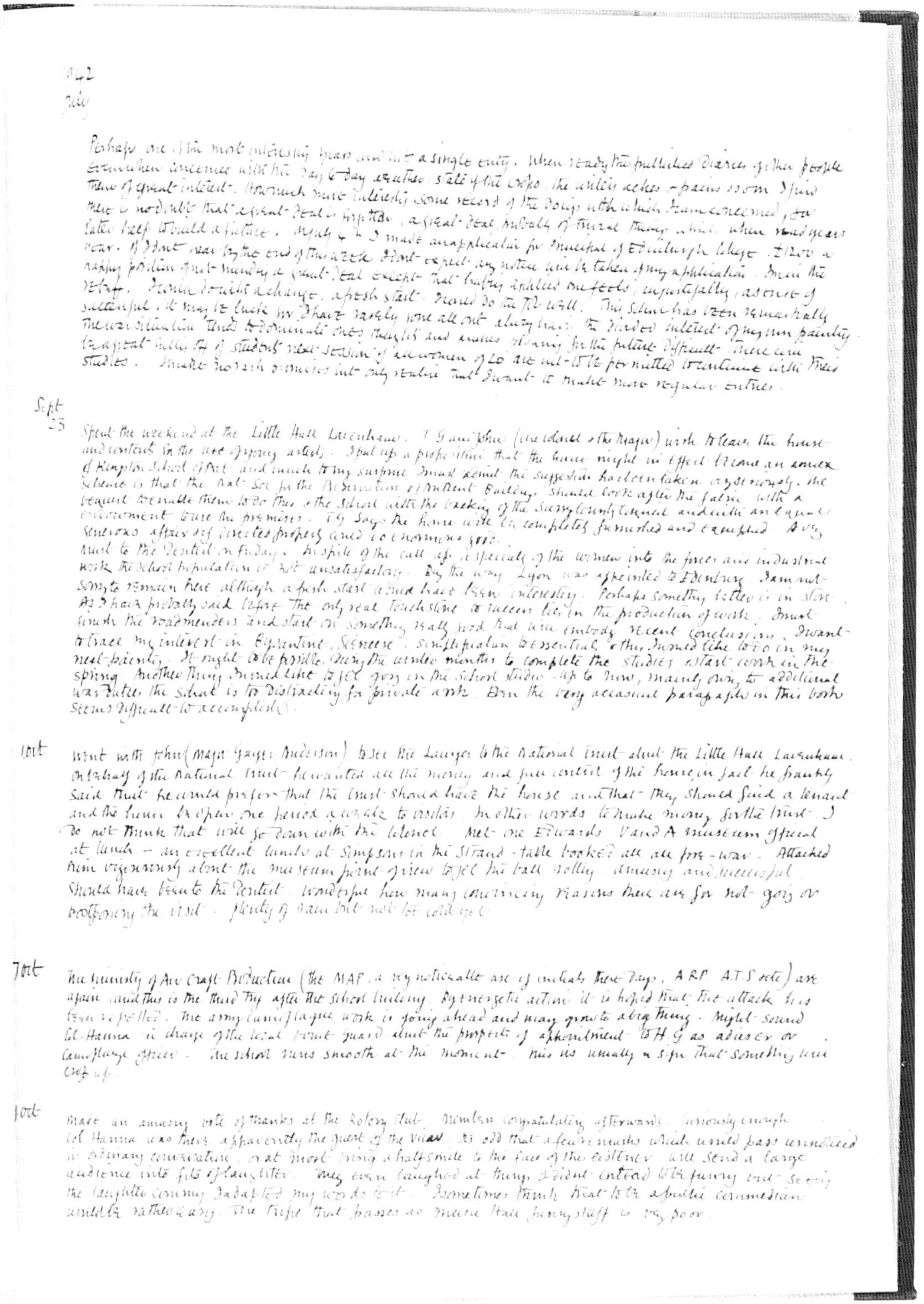

Fig.22 Page from Brill's immaculate handwritten diary (July 1942)

Plate 1. *Self-portrait*. Oil on board 388×337 mm (15¼×13¼ in)

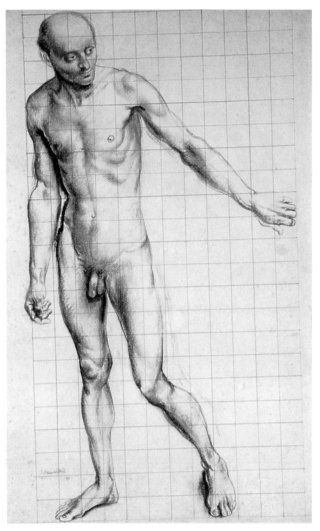

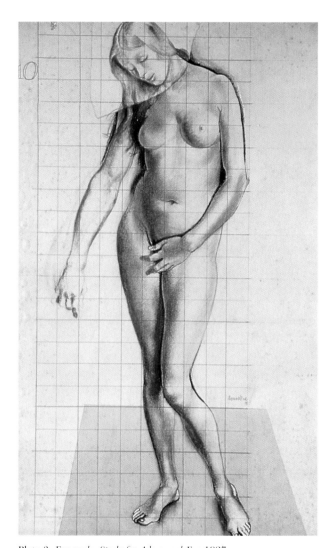

Plate 2. *Adam. Study for Adam and Eve* 1927.
Pencil and pastel 597×355 mm (23½×14 in)

Plate 3. *Eve nude. Study for Adam and Eve* 1927.
Pencil and pastel 610×368 mm (24×14½ in)

Plate 4. *The expulsion of Adam and Eve* 1927. Oil on canvas. See plate 111

Plate 5. *Angel. Study for Adam and Eve* 1927.
Watercolour 444×267 mm (17½×10½ in)

Plate 7. *Palazzo del Priori* 1928. Oil
584×438 mm (23×17¼ in)

Plate 6. *Lincoln Cathedral*. Oil 749×438 mm (29½×17¼ in)

Plate 8. *Boston Stump*. Oil on board 406×267 mm (16×10½ in)

Plate 9. *Buoys at Harwich*. Oil 273×368 mm (10³/₄×14¹/₂ in)

Plate 10. *Buoys II*. Watercolour 248×343 mm (9³/₄×13¹/₂ in)

Plate 11. *Free Press* 1968. Oil on board 279×178 mm (11×7 in)

Plate 12. *Part-time painter* 1967. Oil on board
292×292 mm (11½×11½ in)

Plate 13. *Hole in the road* 1963. Oil on board
343×267 mm (13½×10½ in)

Plate 14. *The waiting room* 1960. Oil on board
1016×1270 mm (40×50 in)

Plate 15. *One for the road* 1963. Oil on board
337×260 mm (13¼×10¼ in)

Plate 16. *Artist in his library*. Pen and wash
483×311 mm (19×12¼ in)

Plate 17. *Man in the library* 1964. Oil on board
305×229 mm (12×9 in)

Plate 18 *Man and girl dancing.* Oil sketch 305×229 mm (12×9 in)

Plate 19. *Sketch for a young woman with red hair.* Watercolour 559×381 mm (22×15 in)

Plate 20. *Portrait of a young woman with red hair.* Oil 610×508 mm (24×20 in)

Plate 21. *The bather.* Painted paper (gouache) mosaic 838×635 mm (33×25 in)

Plate 22. *Young woman in Rome* 1930. Tempera
356×305 mm (14×12 in)

Plate 23. *The pink headscarf* 1930. Oil on board
343×292 mm (13½×11½ in)

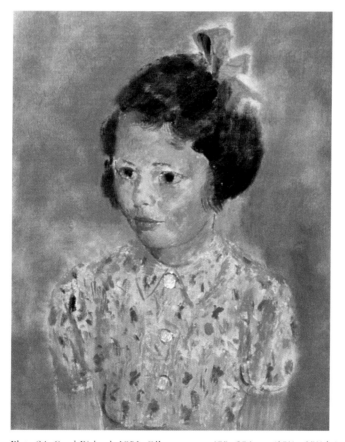

Plate 24. *Carol Richards* 1951. Oil on canvas 495×394mm (19½×15½ in)

Plate 25. *Corn in the hills* c.1934. Oil on canvas 991×1981 mm (39×78 in)

Plate 26. *Nativity at Cockfield* c.1935. Oil on canvas

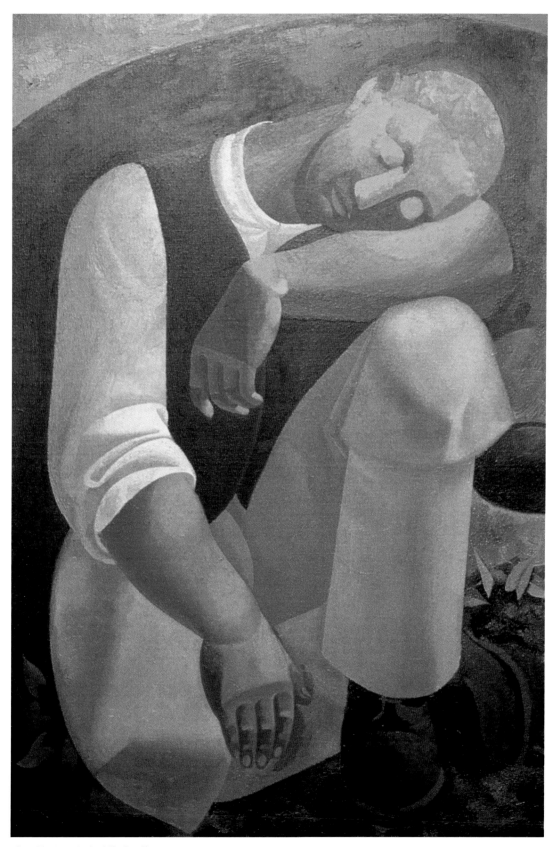

Plate 27. *Corn in the hills* detail

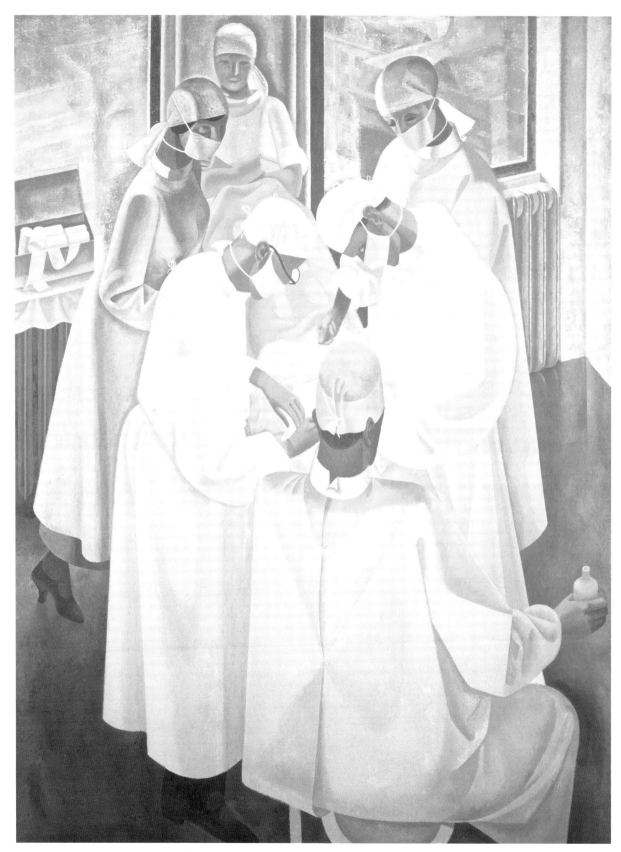

Plate 28. *A surgical operation* 1934–5. Oil on canvas 2050×1600 mm (80¾×63 in)

Plate 29. *Mayoral procession (Kingston Guildhall)*. Oil on canvas 880×1200 mm (34³/₄×47¹/₄ in)

Plate 30. *Two hundred at Lynn* 1969. 552×406 mm (21³⁄₄×16 in)

Plate 31. *Cattle market* 1966. 698×902 mm (27½×35½ in)

Plate 32. *The pig market* 1969. Oil on board 914×711 mm (36×28 in)

Plate 33. *The black bull in the ring* 1966. Oil on board 762×1067 mm (30×42 in)

Plate 34. *The black bull. Sketch*. Pen and wash 216×317 mm (8½×12½ in)

Plate 35. *The black bull in the ring* detail

Plate 36. *The black bull* 1966. Oil on board 381×787 mm (15×31 in)

Plate 37. *The cattle auction* 1966. Oil on board 1118×787 mm (44×31 in)

Plate 38. *The jury* 1960. Oil on board 1219×1422 mm (48×56 in)

Plate 39. *The jury* detail

Plate 40. *Sketch for line men*

Plate 41. *Line men* 1958. Oil on board 2134×1067 mm (84×42 in)

Plate 42. *Coalman at rest c.*1964. Oil on board

Plate 43. *Rest* 1956. Oil on canvas 1700×2150 mm (67×84½ in)

Plate 44. *Football carnival, Market Place, Kingston*. Oil on board 749×1041 mm (29½×41 in)

Plate 45. *Junk* 1963. Oil 762×1016 mm (30×40 in)

31 Dec 1961

Plate 46. *Snow in the garden, 31 December 1961.* Pen and ink (Sketchbook)

Plate 47. *Snow in the garden*. Oil on canvas

Plate 48. *Sketch for a nightmare*. Watercolour 572×381 mm (22½×15 in)

Plate 49. *Nightmare*. Oil 736×482 mm (29×19 in)

Plate 50. *The garden I*. Painted paper (gouache) mosaic 457×610 mm (18×24 in)

Plate 51. *The garden II*. Painted paper (gouache) mosaic 533×750 mm (21×29½ in)

Plate 52. *The gardener*. Painted paper (gouache) mosaic 768×508 mm (30¼×20 in)

Plate 53. *Two windows*. Painted paper (gouache) mosaic 711×812 mm (28×32 in)

Plate 54. *Siena* 1955. Painted paper (gouache) mosaic

Plate 55. *Tree trunks II*. Watercolour 343×521 mm (13½×20½ in)

Plate 56. *Tree trunks I*. Watercolour 343×419 mm (13½×16½ in)

Plate 57. *Log composition*. Watercolour 203×260 mm (8×10¼ in)

Plate 58. *The bridge*. Watercolour 241×343 mm (9½×13½ in)

Plate 59. *Woodlands c.*1935. Watercolour

Plate 60. *Suffolk barn*. Watercolour 267×369 mm (10½×14½ in)

Plate 61. *Haystacks* 1931. Watercolour 368×540 mm (14½×21¼ in)

Plate 62. *Cockfield scene* 1932. Watercolour 330×477 mm (13×18¾ in)

Plate 63. *Welsh scene* 1931. Watercolour 248×350 mm (9¾×13¾ in)

Plate 64. *Rhubarb* 1934. Watercolour

Plate 65. *Artichokes*. Watercolour 362×533 mm (14¹/₁×21 in)

Plate 66. *Muckish I* 1933. Watercolour 292×451 mm (11½×17¾ in)

Plate 67. *Donegal scene* 1933. Watercolour 305×470 mm (12×18½ in)

Plate 68. *Loch*. Watercolour 298×457 mm (11³/₄×18 in)

Plate 69. *Irish landscape* 1933. Watercolour 286×413 mm (11¹/₄×16¹/₄ in)

Plate 70. *The Lakes*. Watercolour 254×349 mm (10×13¾ in)

Plate 71. *Italian scene* 1955. Pen and wash 191×273 mm (7½×10¾ in)

Plate 72. *Tower: Italian scene*. Pen and wash 280×419 mm (11×16½ in)

Plate 73. *Church of San Ruffino, Assisi*. Watercolour, pastel, charcoal, gouache 242×280 mm (9¹/₂×11 in)

Plate 74. *Viterbo* 1929. Pen and wash 267×406 mm (10½×16 in)

Plate 75. *The British School of Rome* 1929. Pen, pencil, crayon 267×343 mm (10½×13½ in)

Plate 76. *Italian church and rooftops.* Pen and wash 305×432 mm (12×17 in)

Plate 77. *Florence*. Pen and wash 305×413 mm (12×16¼ in)

Plate 78. *Cafe Sphinx – street scene in Alexandria, Egypt* 1930. Sepia 350×260 mm (13³/₄×10¹/₄ in)

Plate 79. *The Mosque, Cairo* 1930. Watercolour 413×343 mm (16¼×13½ in)

Plate 80. *Rooftops, Kingston*. Pen and wash 286×394 mm (11¼×15½ in)

Plate 81. *Sketch for family portrait* 1964–5. Pen and watercolour 432×578 mm (17×22¾ in)

Plates 82–85. Selection of illustrated envelopes (wage payments) presented weekly by Brill to his housekeeper, Nellie Smith

Plate 86

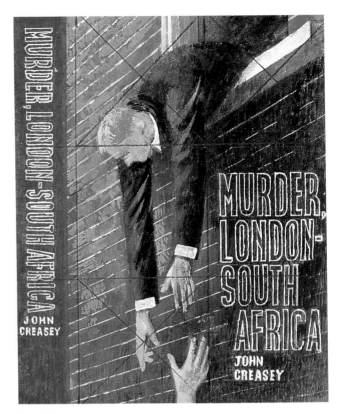

Plate 87

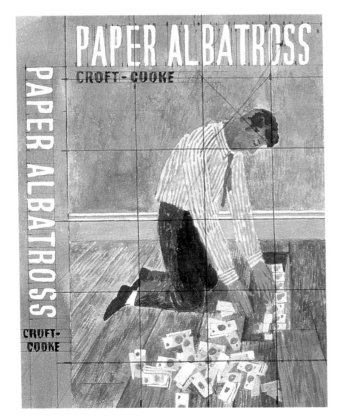

Plate 88

Plate 89

Plate 90. *Awaiting the guests*. Pen and ink 153×191 mm (6×7½ in)

Plate 91. *Orders for the day*. Pen and ink with pencil 153×191 mm (6×7½ in)

Plate 92. *The Bellringer*. Pencil 800×457 mm (31½×18 in)

Plate 93. *The auctioneer* 1966. Pen and ink, approx 229×343 mm (9×13½ in)

Plate 94. *Kingston Market*. Pen and ink

Plate 95. *Mid-day*. Pen and ink 1219×812 mm (48×32 in)

Plate 96. *Harwich*. Pen and wash 210×337 mm (8¼×13¼ in)

Plate 97. *Curing sheds*. Pen and wash 330×483 mm (13×19 in)

Plate 98. *Wisbeach*. Pen and wash 229×318 mm (9×12½ in)

Plate 99. *Wisbeach*. Pen and crayon 438×578 mm (17¼×22¾ in)

Plate 100. *Wisbeach. Harbour scene*. Pen and crayon 438×578 mm (17¼×22¾ in)

Plate 101. *Italian scene*. Pen and wash 305×457 mm (12×18 in)

Plate 102. *Bologna* 1951. Pen and wash 305×464 mm (12×18¼ in)

Plate 103. *Italian villa in the hills.* Pen and wash 432×623 mm (17×24½ in)

Plate 104. *Mountains. Italy.* Pen and wash 305×445 mm (12×17½ in)

Plate 105. *Irish hills*. Pen and wash 439×699 mm (17¼×27½ in)

Plate 106. *Italian villas*. Pen and wash 298×394 mm (11¾×15½ in)

Plate 107. *Hills beyond the towns*. Pen and wash 552×1137 mm (21¾×44¾ in)

Plate 108. *Flower studies*. Watercolour 381×559 mm (15×22 in)

Plate 109. *Study of ivy*. Pen and wash 305×457 mm (12×18 in)

Plate 110. *Grasses*. Ink and charcoal 268×400 mm (10½×15¾ in)

Plate 111. *Tree* 1927. Pen and wash 514×305 mm (20¼×12 in). See plate 4

Plate 112. *The balcony*. Ink and wash 737×438 mm (29×17¼ in)

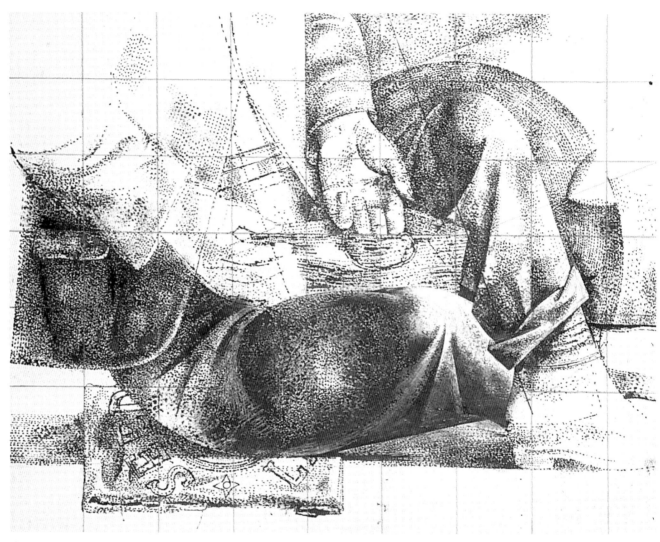

Plate 113. *Study of a workman*. Pen and wash 305×387 mm (12×15 in)

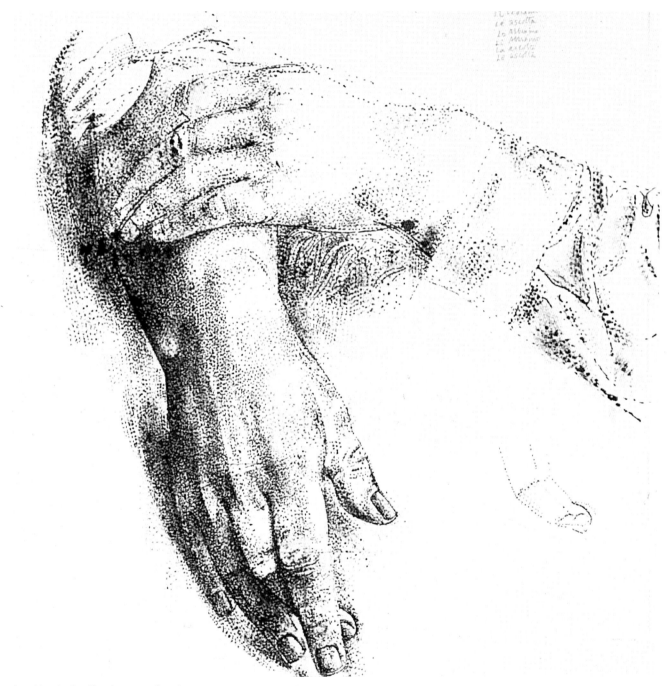

Plate 114. *Study of hands*. Pen and wash 305×311 mm (12×12¼ in)

Plate 115. *Path in the woods*. Pen and wash 305×394 mm (12×15½ in)

Plate 116. *Man reclining – squared sketch c.*1963. Pen 381×419 mm (15×16¹/₂ in)

Plate 117. *Sketch for a painting on reverse of 'A surgical operation'* (plate 28). *c.*1928

Plate 118. *Workmen in trench*

Plate 119. *Four men looking at hole in the road*

Plate 120. *The Nightwatchman*

Plate 121. *Woman in turban (Rosalie Brill)*

Plate 122. *Woman in turban, with additional figure sketched in.* Pencil over photograph 110×83 mm (4¼×3¼ in)

Plate 123. *Self-portrait, Rome.* 387×349 mm (15¼×13¾ in)

Plate 124. *Head of a young man*. Pen and crayon 292×210 mm (11¹/₂×8¹/₄ in)

Plate 125. *Girl with head in hand (Rosalie Brill)*. Pencil

Plate 126. *Woman seated*. Pencil 343×222 mm (13½×8¾ in)

Plate 127. *Carol Richards* 1953. Ink 419×267 mm (16½×10½ in)

Plate 128. *Knitting* 1960. Pen and wash 584×432 mm (23×17 in)

Plate 129. *Sketch for 'Patience'*. Watercolour 578×318 mm (22³⁄₄×12¹⁄₂ in)

Plate 130. *Tea for two*. Watercolour 381×508 mm (15×20 in)

Plate 131. *David Brill*. Pen and wash 381×178 mm (15×7 in)

Plate 132. *The breakfast table*. Pencil 140×457 mm (5¹/₂×18 in)

Plate 133. *Window cleaner*. Pencil and white paint 229×292 mm (9×11¹/₂ in)

Plate 134. *Head of a girl* 1950. Pen and ink 495×590 mm (19½×23¼ in)

Chronology

6 May 1902
Reginald Brill born in Hither Green, London

1917-18
Attended evening classes at St Martin's School of Art

1920
Awarded LCC scholarship to Slade School of Fine Art

1920-23
At Slade under Professor Tonks

1922-24
Employed at Stoke Rochford Hall by Christopher Hatton Turnor: mural painting

12 October 1925
Married Rosalie Clarke at Fulham Register Office

1925-27
Freelance employment on *Lansbury's Labour Weekly*

1927
Won Rome Prize in Decorative Painting

1927-29
Scholar, British School at Rome

1929
Taught at Blackheath School of Art

1930
Spent six months in Egypt at invitation of government
Met Major Robert Gayer-Anderson
Painted city, landscapes and the Nile
Returned to England via the Greek Islands and Italy

1933
Appointed Head Master of Kingston School of Art

1 January 1934
Took up appointment at Kingston
Embarked on programme of substantial paintings on a common theme ('Martyrdom of Man')

1937
Brills moved from Fulham to 6B Palace Road, Kingston

12 October 1939
School of Art moved to new purpose-built premises in Knights Park

1940
Brills moved to 1 Crescent Road, Kingston Hill

1941
Undertook fire-watching duties at School of Art

1942
Visited Gayer-Anderson brothers at Lavenham, Suffolk. Discussed possibility of their family home, Little Hall, being bequeathed to Surrey County Council for the benefit of young artists, perhaps as an annexe for Kingston School of Art

1946
Published *Modern Painting and its Roots in European tradition*

1951
Brill's *Seaside Promenade* one of several murals mounted by staff and students at the Festival of Britain

1952
Painted Kingston's mayor, town clerk and macebearer in procession at Proclamation of Queen Elizabeth II

1955
Initiated scheme for Kingston Council to commission artists to paint local views (now known as the Brill Collection)

1959
Appeared on BBC TV 'Monitor' programme with the artist Keith Grant and Malcolm Kador, both also at the school, to discuss what students hoped to gain by attending art school

1960
Death of Colonel T. G. Gayer-Anderson
Brill visited Lavenham to discuss transfer of Little Hall

1961
Opening of £100,000 extension to Kingston School of Art by Sir Charles Wheeler, President of the Royal Academy

1962
Published *Art as a Career*
Retired as Principal of Kingston School of Art, to be succeeded by Wilfred Fairclough
Moved to Lavenham to become Warden of Little Hall

25 May 1974
Retrospective exhibition at the Phoenix Gallery, Lavenham

14 June 1974
Died at Little Hall

Plate 135. *Self-portrait* (from final sketchbook). Pen and ink

Fig.23 1962 Ink

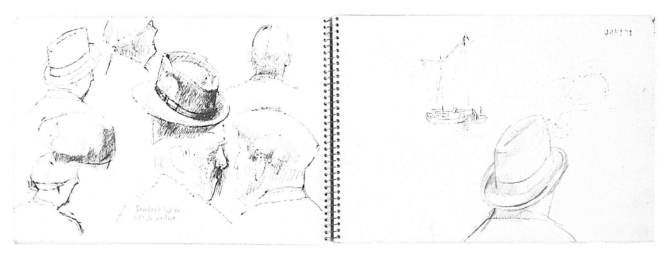

Fig.24 1966 Ink, pencil

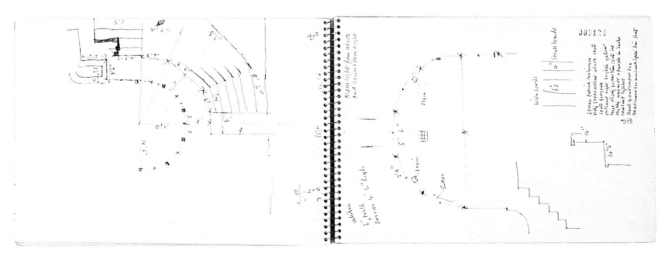

Fig.25 1966 Ink and biro. Floor plan and measurements of auction ring for *The Cattle Auction* (plate 37)

Selection taken from over nine sketchbooks, 1955-68

134

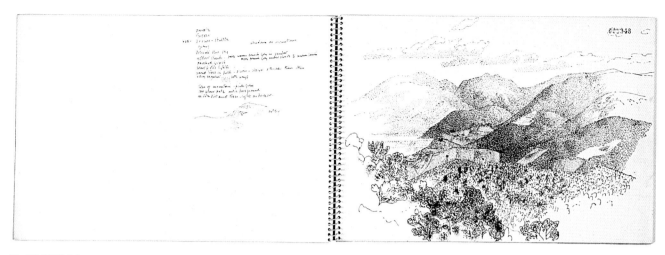

Fig.26 1962 Ink

Fig.27 (no date) Ink

Fig.28 1964 Ink

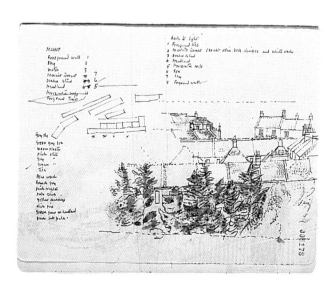

Fig.29 1956 Ink and crayon

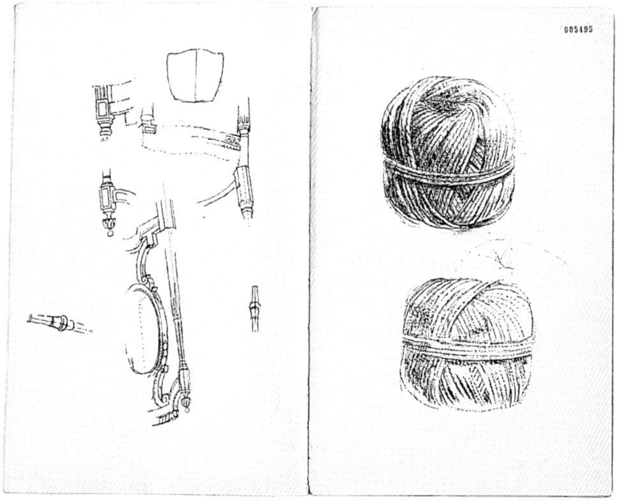

Fig.30 1960 Ink

Figs 31, 32 *Workers of the World arise* and *'but we must cultivate our garden'*,
two from a series of four illustrations commissioned by Lloyds Bank,
1957 and 1958 (whereabouts of the originals unknown)

Reginald Brill

"but we must cultivate our garden"

(*Candide*)

Thinking seriously about things – and what better place to do this than in a receptive wheelbarrow on a mild Autumnal day – one realises the truth of this maxim of Candide's.

Our gardens must be cultivated with a steady assiduity and with special knowledge if they are to develop and fructify.

So with the business of Lloyds Bank : we pride ourselves on providing our many customers with an informed and courteous service on all financial matters – the essence of the cultivation of prosperity.

LLOYDS BANK LIMITED

Recollections of Kingston and Brill

The teacher: Les Duxbury

Reginald Brill had quite a distinguished presence – he would now be called charismatic. He was a tall, upright man, who with his beard and air of nonchalance looked the part of the slightly bohemian artist. He was a Rome Scholar, which qualified him as a cultured European. His manner and authority were similar to his contemporaries in like situations; a lot of autonomy and autocratic bearing, products of post-World War One scepticism and conceit.

Brill was a favourite of, and wholeheartedly supported by, Mrs Bidmead, the then chairman of Kingston Education Authority, and herself a formidable and progressive Yorkshirewoman from Hull. With her support, Brill was able to direct his school by delegation, reserving his post as boss with dignity. He was affable, had a ready wit, and was liked by, and more or less respected by, his staff and most of the students. He was sociable, with an urbane charm. Along with Wilfred Fairclough, who was to succeed him as Principal of what was then the Kingston School of Art, he was a member of the Chelsea Arts Club and about once a week they went on a mild spree. The sight of Brill and Fairclough strolling together along the Kings Road, Chelsea, was worthy of a cartoon by Max Beerbohm. Often, part-time staff were recruited from this source; for example Stanley Ayers, John Newton, Clarence Mirfield and Fred Heyworth. Brill's wife, Rosalie, was an elegant lady. She looked a bit like one of Augustus John's women – Madame Suggia, or Dorelia.

As a painter, Brill's own work was somewhat catholic in subject matter, mostly objective and with a decorative quality in his studied compositions. He did a lot of drawing which he altered and worked up into the final composition, which was then squared up and transferred to canvas. He was a competent technician as painter and draughtsman. Later in his career he was commissioned to do some pen drawings for Lloyds Bank and his technique displayed a lot of regular dotted lines (rather like the roulette effect in an etching), a convention he had adopted years before, but we, his staff at Kingston, firmly maintained he had been given for Christmas a dot-making machine (see Figs 16, 17).

Brill's figures were tightly controlled, some of them seeming to derive from Mark Gertler and William Roberts. For the Festival of Britain, in 1951, he worked on a mosaic with John Binns, Head of Interior Design at Kingston. He produced an excellent cartoon for this which had a statuesque quality, with an element of reference to Picasso's Classical period, but owing still more to Gertler. The Binns/Brill project employed Kingston art students unashamedly. After all they were studying the business and welcomed experience. A few of the girls sampled the Brill experience as a bonus.

A singular picture of Brill's was of mural proportions. This was a painting of an operation in an hospital operating theatre, apparently Guy's Hospital, in 1935. It was more austere than his usual compositions, flat planes corresponding with surgeons' gowns, reminiscent of Henry Lamb. This painting has a strange history; it seems to have been displayed somewhere in Kingston School of Art before Brill's retirement and then mislaid. It mysteriously resurfaced, after Kingston Technical College and the Art College combined to form Kingston Polytechnic, strangely located in the Engineers' venue in Canbury Park annexe. The maintenance staff there used it several times to cordon off corridors while at their work, to block up broken windows, and on one occasion even threw it into a skip with the refuse. It was rescued, and hung high above a side entrance where it remained for some years until reclaimed for Brill's retrospective exhibition at Knights Park, where it was sold for a high price. It now hangs in the Wellcome Institute Library in Euston Road.

This retrospective exhibition in 1985 was proof of the wide range of Brill's interest. It showed his love of Italy where he was a frequent visitor, and his interest in the mundane: workmen, farmers, auctions and the like. Mrs Bidmead, in her nineties, attended this show and was loud in praise of her protégé, still applauding his lifelong allegiance to his Lansbury kind of socialism. However, somewhat earlier in his career, this relationship had been tested by a classic case of Brill's waywardness, which occurred during World War Two. Air-raid precautions demanded that all public premises should remain open and that all staff (and sometimes students) should keep a rota of fire-watching overnight. This was a golden opportunity for Reggie Brill, who arranged the rota. He had his eye on a young, glamorous, energetic woman. Mrs Brill learned of these arrangements and was not best pleased, as she knew of Reggie's predilection for the ladies. In my experience, I disturbed him in his Principal's studio in compromising positions with the better-looking female staff and girl students on several occasions. He always reacted calmly and remained unflustered.

The end of his teaching career, in 1962, was gilded by a stewardship ideally suited to his style. Two brothers, the Gayer-Andersons, whom he had met on a visit to Egypt in the 1930s and who had kept in touch with him over the years, founded a Trust and, with Brill as incumbent, a fine old house in Lavenham (Suffolk) with spacious grounds was appointed as a residence for groups of students from Kingston and the Slade to spend several weeks working in the country and experiencing gracious living. A cellar was laid down to Brill's liking, servants appointed, and Mr and Mrs Brill moved in, immediately on his retirement from Kingston. It was a sinecure. Students went and went again. They didn't exactly dress for dinner, but they washed their hands and some even wore ties. It was good while it lasted, but the gilding was tarnished by a change in administration which relieved Brill of his warden's post in 1971, leaving him with bleak and bitter prospects until his death in 1974.

To sum up Brill's character and achievements – that's impossible and unnecessary. There are sufficient testimonies and tributes from those who knew him, and enough evidence of the works he left, to confirm his status as an artist, a teacher, and as a man.

The student: Alan Bartram

I'm never very good with dates, but it must have been autumn 1949 when I became a student at Kingston School of Art. In those days, art education was logical and straight-forward. The first two years were spent on the Intermediate Course, which covered almost anything you could think of in the field of visual arts, and crafts too. The core of it was drawing, particularly life drawing, from which all aesthetic principles could be discovered. You studied architecture by seriously drawing local buildings (Hampton Court is not far away). You studied anatomy, perspective, sculpture, 'basic design' (fashionable at the time), lettering, calligraphy, graphic design (possibly then the weakest department at Kingston); you researched and illustrated (with your own drawings) subjects such as the history of architecture, or furniture. While we were never required to design a building, we had talks by teachers from the lively and highly respected Architecture School in the same building. And of course you painted, although this was always slightly oddly called figure composition (and done with poster paints – more difficult to handle, though cheaper, than oils). And endless sketching. Just down the road was Kingston Market with (I think) a weekly cattle market; so we did a lot of drawings just like those of Mr Brill – though far less competent.

After two years on the Intermediate Course, you special-ised for another two years: painting, sculpture, stained glass, whatever. It seemed to me then, and it seems to me now, an extremely good system.

The building itself, built in 1939, was banal; but, possibly more by good luck than good judgement, it worked. The building is arranged around a grassed central space, like a cloister. The symbolism escaped me at the time, but we certainly needed a monk-like dedication to master that course. Corridors ran all round this space. Studios, common room, offices and so on opened off these corridors; along the walls were lockers. They were of a convenient height and size for jumping up and sitting on, legs dangling; and during the breaks from life drawing, we came out of the studios to do just that, or lean out of the windows to watch sculpture students hacking at lumps of stone in the courtyard below, or loll around generally, and chatter. In the summer lunch hours, the grassy bank running down to the small Hogsmill River, on the sunny side of the building, would be dotted with students lazing around. Real life was earnest, after grammar school or whatever, but also enjoyable. It seems to me that Mr Brill, scarcely visible behind the scenes (and even when sighted, half-hidden by his bushy beard), ran a rather happy ship. Like Alan Bennett, I have never been noted for my *joie de vivre*; but I think my time there was possibly the happiest four years of my life. It was a very good school.

Although Mr Brill gave the occasional crit, one of his more notable skills as Principal must have been choosing his staff. The Vice-Principal was Mr Fairclough, a Lancashire man and a slightly dry old stick – if his rather podgy form can be described that way. His teaching, if a little solemn, was never a tired formula and always showed a personal interest in each student. By chance, in 1990 I designed a book of his etchings (also published by Scolar). Mr Brill had a sharp eye for character and oddities, as can be seen in our illustrations; but Mr Fairclough possessed this to the nth degree. It was conveyed in his prints by the amazingly controlled drawing (another characteristic shared with Mr Brill) and sheer technical brilliance. We were not properly aware of this at the time.

For me, Mr Brill's most effective act was his bold pairing of the two principal painting teachers. Mr Archer was cultivated, elegant (he reminded me for some reason of the younger, unbearded, Ruskin) and unflaggingly enthusiastic. If he could not get you interested in a subject, no-one could. He was a brilliant teacher. He was the one who taught us all the 'boring' academic stuff; design, structure, colour, drawing, observation, technique; even history of art was slipped in painlessly. Mr Newton, on the other hand, was more of the let-it-all-hang-out school. A Sunderland man with a Joe Stalin (then) or a Saddam (now) moustache, he had an earthy sense of humour and was altogether a blunter and more matey kind of chap. It might be thought that such contrasting characters would confuse the students, but that was not the case. You could take the restrained expressionism of Mr Newton (who would tell you what he was currently at work on, and the feelings he was trying to express – which was just as influential as if he had shown you the painting; perhaps more so, and less likely to lead to plagiarism). You could marry it, in your own way, with Mr Archer's teaching which, although essentially academic, never seemed so at the time.

Unlikely pairing it might have been, but it worked. *Good* on you, Mr Brill.

In my time, the Painting School had an annexe in a tall early-Victorian house opposite Kingston Station. Some of us would go for tea break with Mr Newton in the nearby caff decorated, as he described it, in custard and cabbage water. Even then we never called him 'John'. As my four years at Kingston were coming to an end, he asked me my plans.

When I told him I was going to do graphic design, he was discouraging. 'You need time to lean over the bridge and spit in the water, and you won't get it doing that.' Fortunately, despite sometimes coming under pressure in the way designers do, I've always been able to do some painting. And today, fifty years on, I often think of the teaching I got at Kingston with respect – and gratitude. Yes: a very good school.

Fig.33 Celebrating the opening of the 1961 extension

Fig.34 Brill at work

Fig.35 Party held on the occasion of the opening of the extension
to Kingston School of Art, October 1961. Front right: Reginald Brill,
Rosalie Brill and Frank Archer. Behind Mr Archer, Sir Charles Wheeler

List of illustrations

Figures

Author's Acknowledgements

In researching this book I am indebted in the first instance to Reginald Brill's nephews and nieces and their families, who provided personal insights and documentary evidence: to Carol and the late Dr David Richards, the late John Webb, David and Vera Brill, Jane Merchant, Eira Gill and Katrina Donaldson. Sadly, David Richards and John Webb died while this book was in preparation.

Without the generous help of Brill's friends and acquaintances, and the staff and students of Kingston School of Art, who with their vivid recall have helped me flesh out the man and the artist, I should not have been able to write this book. I am immensely grateful to the following witnesses: Dennis Berry, Lorna Binns, Daphne Brooker, Max Brooker, Robert Brown, John Carter, Lena Cooke, Sally Dray, Leslie Duxbury, Joan Fairclough, Michael Fairclough, George Faiers, Pam Forster, Joyce Gardner, Eric Geddis, Ann Gurling, Penelope Gretton, Sydney Hall, Reginald Hanson, Marjorie Hindley, Constance Howard, Keith Hutchinson, Philip Kemp, Tony Leach, Joe Ledger, William Ledger, Jeff McCormack, Mary Malenoir, Leonard Manasseh, Charles Marriott, Dr Alan Matterson, Gordon Miller, John Mitchell, Don Pavey, Charles Potts, Mick Rooney, Leonard Rosoman, Nellie Smith, Judith Waters, Mavis Wrightson.

Brill's first visit to Italy as a Rome Scholar remained inspirational. As the British School at Rome Archive is currently closed to scholars I owe a great debt to Paul Liss and Dr Alan Powers for the loan of documents, to Peyton Skipwith for research generously carried out on my behalf at the School, and to Professor Andrew Wallace-Hadrill, Valerie Scott, Librarian, Stephen Farthing, Professor Paul Huxley and Ian Tregarthen Jenkin for their assistance.

I should like to give special thanks to the following who provided much valued information: Dr Mark Attew, Mary Axon, Margaret Bird, Sylvia Blanc, Dr Emma Chambers, Cyril and Joyce Cheshire, Professor Bernard Cohen, James and Graham Connell, Diana Darrer, Adrian de Peyer, David and Richard de Peyer, David Drummond, Ray and Audrey Emeney, Henry Engleheart, William Feaver, David Gurling, Marylyn Gurling, James Gorst, Joseph P. Hamer, James and Lavender Hawkins, Christopher Hawkins, Paul Hetherington, Susan Kent, Margaret King, A. B. Leach, Gregory Luton, Anne McCormack, Alasdair and Rosemary McCorquodale, Dennis Marks, Alfred and Helen Mignano, Mary Mitchell, Edward Morgan, Gerald and Judy Moriarty, Keith New, Sir Duncan Oppenheim, Dr Colin Painter, John Popham, Pamela Richardson, Peter Robinson, Professor Ian Rogerson, Ian I. Rosenblatt, Richard Scott, Marion Shipley, Dr Robert Smith, June Sampson, William Schupbach, John Smith, Michael Stainton, Nicholas Tavener, Adrian and Jane Thorpe, John Vockings, John Wynne-Williams, Professor R. B. Welbourn, Clive and Shirley Woodham, Luciano Zucchi.

Among the many curators, librarians and archivists who have offered me help I must thank in particular Renée Attew, Hugh Belsey, Rosamund Cummings, Christine Hopper, Vicky Isley, Dr Zdzisław Jagodziński, Alan Kent, Anne Lutyens-Humfrey, Graham Patrick, Mark Pomeroy, Neil Rhind, Karen Sampson, Anna Sienkiewiczowa.

Lastly, I must thank my husband Bernard Bumpus for practical help with research and for his unflagging support and encouragement.

Judith Bumpus
March 1999

University's Acknowledgements

Kingston University wishes to thank all who have so generously contributed to the fascinating research carried out so thoroughly by Judith Bumpus to produce this, the first book on Reginald Brill.

We would also like to thank Kingstonian Football Club, Kingston Guildhall, Philip Sober, the Tate Gallery, Wellcome Institute Library and Robert Whittaker.

Although already mentioned elsewhere, Carol Richards's relentless support and enthusiasm for the entire Brill Project have proved invaluable.

Noel Oddy, of Highgate Fine Art, with suggestions of leads to follow, unflagging energy and in particular depth of knowledge of and admiration for Brill's work, has provided constant inspiration and back-up for the publication of this book and accompanying exhibitions.

Leo Duff
March 1999

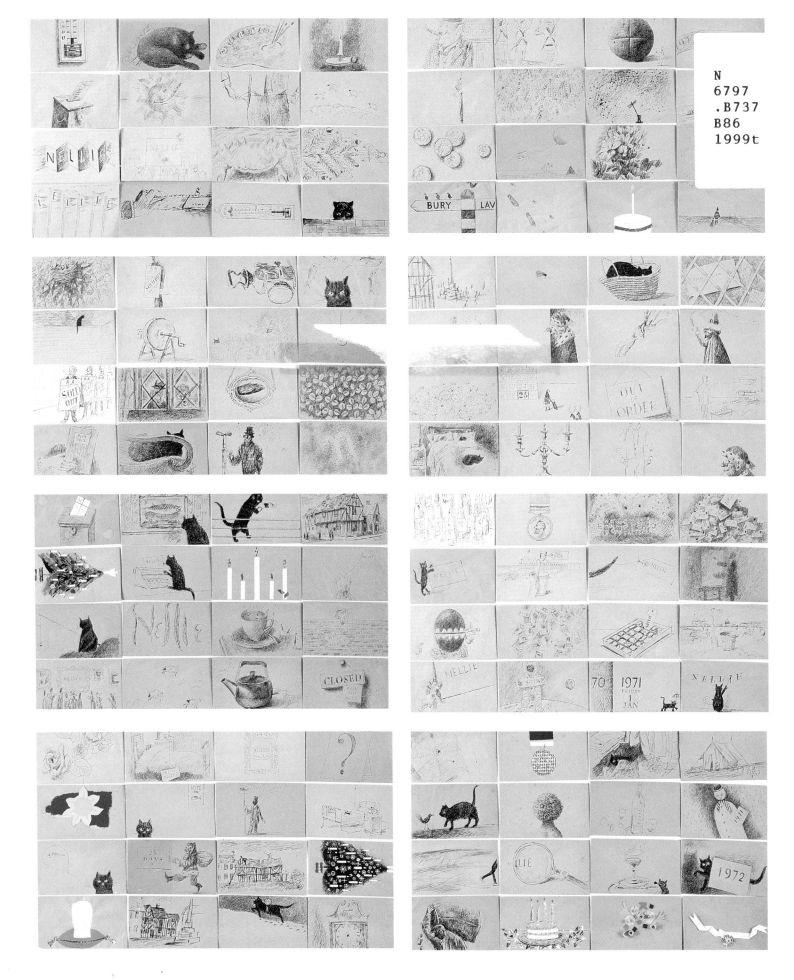

N
6797
.B737
B86
1999t